THE GUYS AND DOLLS BOOK

Julia McKenzie as Miss Adelaide in the National Theatre production, 1982

THE GUYS AND DOLLS BOOK

Frank Loesser

Joe Swerling

Abe Burrows

Damon Runyon

Caryl Brahms

Ned Sherrin

Russell Davies

and Richard Eyre

with National Theatre production photos by
John Haynes.

A Methuen Paperback
in association with the National Theatre, London

methuen

L O N D O N

THE GUYS AND DOLLS BOOK

A Methuen Paperback
The Guys and Dolls Book first published as a Methuen
Paperback in 1982 by Methuen London Ltd, 11 New
Fetter Lane, London EC4P 4EE.

Guys and Dolls: Book by Jo Swerling. Lyrics by Frank
Loesser. Copyright 1951 and 1960 by Frank Loesser, Jo
Swerling, and Abe Burrows. Reprinted here by
arrangement with Harold Orenstein, 110 West 57th
Street, New York, NY 10019, USA. Frank Loesser's
lyrics included in this edition by arrangement with
Chappell Morris Ltd, 129 Park Street, London W1Y
3FA.

'The Idyll of Miss Sarah Brown' by Damon Runyon
copyright © 1954-1975. Reprinted by arrangement with
Constable Publishers.

'Frank Loesser' by Caryl Brahms and Ned Sherrin
copyright © 1982 by Caryl Brahms and Ned Sherrin. First
appeared as 'Blow by Blow by Frank Loesser' in *Drama*.

'Directing Guys and Dolls' by Richard Eyre copyright ©
1982 by Richard Eyre. First published in this volume.

'The National Theatre production reviewed' by Russell
Davies copyright © 1982 by Russell Davies. First
appeared in *Plays and Players*. Reprinted by permission.

Cover design based on the National Theatre programme
and poster designed and illustrated by Richard Bird.
Book design Peter Bennett.

ISBN 0 413 51760 8

Printed in Great Britain by
Blantyre Printing and Binding Ltd,
London and Glasgow

THE GUYS AND DOLLS BOOK

Contents

The Idyll of Miss Sarah Brown
by Damon Runyon   9

Frank Loesser
by Caryl Brahms and Ned Sherrin   21

Directing the National Theatre *Guys and Dolls*
by Richard Eyre   34

The National Theatre production reviewed
by Russell Davies   39

GUYS AND DOLLS
complete book and lyrics   44

In the autumn of 1982 there were the following cast changes to the
National Theatre production:

SARAH	Belinda Sinclair
NATHAN DETROIT	Trevor Peacock
SKY MASTERSON	Paul Jones
HOT HORSE HERBIE	Vincent Pickering
SKY ROCKET	Ian Bartholomew
MARTHA/HOT BOX GIRL	Gail Rolfe
HOT BOX GIRL	Carol Ball

Illustrations
All the National Theatre production photos are by John Haynes.
Sources for the other illustrations are:
The Raymond Mander and Joe Mitchenson Theatre Collection:
page nos. 6, 7 (top), 8, 22, 23, 26, 27, 28, 31, 41
The Cinema Bookshop: page nos. 13, 32–3, 35, 36, 38
The British Theatre Association: page nos. 29, 30
The National Theatre: page nos. 42–3

Edmund Hockridge and Lizbeth Webb (*top*), Sky and Sarah in the 1953 London production, and (*below*) the National Theatre's first Sky and Sarah, Ian Charleson and Julie Covington

Damon Runyon

Alfred Damon Runyon, born in Kansas and a stranger to Manhattan until he was 26, lived and died a New Yorker. He had the native curiosity of a writer, and this, coupled with his New York surroundings, made him easy prey early in his career for the Broadwayite's disease — being in the middle of the news when it is being made. You see them in Lindy's or Reuben's or Gallagher's — young-old souls, quick-taiking and nervous — and their conversation always is of the things of the hour . . . the big fight coming up tomorrow, the newest television sensation, the coming two-year-old colt. The password, always, is "What's new?"

It was that way with Runyon until the day he died. Most of New York knows by now that he fell victim to cancer of the throat. In the last months of his life, he couldn't talk, or at best he could whisper hoarsely. It didn't make a single difference in Runyon's way of life. With his throat muffled up and a pad and pencil always in his pocket, he continued to "make the rounds." You would see him sitting in the Stork with Winchell, or hovering over the coffee in Lindy's, and so on. He knew where he was headed, but it didn't matter. He wanted to be where the news was being made, where they were answering the question "What's new?"

Runyon was a reserved man, with many acquaintances and few close friends. He was the son of an itinerant printer and at 14 he fought in the Spanish-American War. He began his newspaper career on the Pueblo, Colo., Chieftain and he came first to New York in 1910 to publicize a convention of electric-light executives. He only needed one taste of the big town. A year later the New York American hired him, and almost from the beginning — which was sports writing — he was a success.

Always he was where the big story was. He was a correspondent overseas during the Argonne and Meuse campaigns in the first World War. He wrote of Black Jack Pershing's chase of Pancho Villa through Mexico. He didn't miss a heavyweight boxing championship bout in thirty years, right back to Johnson-Willard at Havana.

Runyon needed more money than his newspaper salary. He started writing fiction, taking the Broadway crowd and squeezing them into shapes even more grotesque than their own. Collier's started printing them — and they swept the country. "I took one little section of New York and made a half a million writing about it," he liked to recall. Before long, the movies bit — and "Lady for a Day," "Little Miss Marker," "A Slight Case of Murder," "The Lemon Drop Kid" and others came to life on the silver-plated screen. "Guys and Dolls" is the first musical culled from Runyon material to reach the stage.

As for the love scene along his beloved Broadway — Runyon had one of his characters sum it up thus, once:

"When a guy is knocking around Broadway as long as The Brain, he is bound to accumulate dolls here and there, but most guys accumulate one at a time, and when this one runs out on him, as Broadway dolls will do, he accumulates another, and so on, and so on, until he is too old to care about such matters as dolls, which is when he is maybe a hundred and four years old, although I hear of several guys who beat even this record."

UBLISHED BY
SUPERIOR SOUVENIR BOOK CO
CARE OF KAL EFRON

THE IDYLL OF MISS SARAH BROWN

by Damon Runyon

Of all the high players this country ever sees, there is no doubt but that the guy they call The Sky is the highest. In fact, the reason he is called The Sky is because he goes so high when it comes to betting on any proposition whatever. He will bet all he has, and nobody can bet any more than this.

His right name is Obadiah Masterson, and he is originally out of a little town in southern Colorado where he learns to shoot craps, and play cards, and one thing and another, and where his old man is a very well-known citizen, and something of a sport himself. In fact, The Sky tells me that when he finally cleans up all the loose scratch around his home town and decides he needs more room, his old man has a little private talk with him and says to him like this:

'Son,' the old guy says, 'you are now going out into the wide, wide world to make your own way, and it is a very good thing to do, as there are no more opportunities for you in this burg. I am only sorry,' he says, 'that I am not able to bank-roll you to a very large start, but,' he says, 'not having any potatoes to give you, I am now going to stake you to some very valuable advice, which I personally collect in my years of experience around and about, and I hope and trust you will always bear this advice in mind.

'Son,' the old guy says, 'no matter how far you travel, or how smart you get, always remember this: Some day, somewhere,' he says, 'a guy is going to come to you and show you a nice brand-new deck of cards on which the seal is never broken, and this guy is going to offer to bet you that the jack of spades will jump out of this deck and squirt cider in your ear. But, son,' the old guy says, 'do not bet him, for as sure as you do you are going to get an ear full of cider.'

Well, The Sky remembers what his old man says, and he is always very cautious about betting on such propositions as the jack of spades jumping out of a sealed deck of cards and squirting cider in his ear, and so he makes few mistakes as he goes along. In fact, the only real mistake The Sky makes is when he hits St. Louis after leaving his old home town, and loses all his potatoes betting a guy St. Louis is the biggest town in the world.

Now of course this is before The Sky ever sees any bigger towns, and he is never much of a hand for reading up on matters such as this. In fact, the only reading The Sky ever does as he goes along through life is in these Gideon Bibles such as he finds in the hotel rooms where he lives, for The Sky never lives anywhere else but in hotel rooms for years.

He tells me that he reads many items of great interest in these Gideon Bibles, and furthermore The Sky says that several times these Gideon Bibles keep him from getting out of line, such as the time he finds himself pretty much frozen-in over in Cincinnati, what with owing everybody in town except maybe the mayor from playing games of chance of one kind and another.

Well, The Sky says he sees no way of meeting these obligations and he is figuring the only thing he can do is to take a run-out powder, when he happens to read in one of these Gideon Bibles where it says like this:

'Better is it,' the Gideon Bible says, 'that thou shouldest not vow, than that thou shouldest vow and not pay.'

Well, The Sky says he can see that there is no doubt whatever but that this means a guy shall not welsh, so he remains in Cincinnati until he manages to wiggle himself out of the situation, and from that day to this, The Sky never thinks of welshing.

He is maybe thirty years old, and is a tall guy with a round kisser, and big blue eyes, and he always looks as innocent as a little baby. But The Sky is by no means as innocent as he looks. In fact, The Sky is smarter than three Philadelphia lawyers, which makes him very smart, indeed, and he is well established as a high player in New Orleans, and Chicago, and Los Angeles, and wherever else there is any action in the way of card-playing, or crap-shooting, or horse-racing, or betting on the baseball games, for The Sky is always moving around the country following the action.

But while The Sky will be on anything whatever, he is more of a short-card player and a crap-shooter than anything else, and furthermore he is a great hand for propositions, such as are always coming up among citizens who follow games of chance for a living. Many citizens prefer betting on propositions to anything you can think of, because they figure a proposition gives them a chance to out-smart somebody, and in fact I know citizens who will sit up all night making up propositions to offer other citizens the next day.

A proposition may be only a problem in cards, such as what is the price against a guy getting aces back-to-back, or how often a pair of deuces will win a hand in stud, and then again it may be some very daffy proposition, indeed, although the daffier any proposition seems to be, the more some citizens like it. And no one ever sees The Sky when he does not have some proposition of his own.

The first time he ever shows up around this town, he goes to a baseball game at the Polo Grounds with several prominent citizens, and while he is at the ball game, he buys himself a sack of Harry Stevens' peanuts, which he dumps in a side pocket of his coat.

He is eating these peanuts all through the game, and after the game is over and he is walking across the field with the citizens, he says to them like this:

'What price,' The Sky says, 'I cannot throw a peanut from second base to the home plate?'

Well, everybody knows that a peanut is too light for anybody to throw it this far, so Big Nig, the crap shooter, who always likes to have a little the best of it running for him, speaks as follows:

'You can have 3 to 1 from me, stranger,' Big Nig says.

'Two C's against six,' The Sky says, and then he stands on second base, and takes a peanut out of his pocket, and not only whips it to the home plate, but on into the lap of a fat guy who is still sitting in the grand stand putting the zing on Bill Terry for not taking Walker out of the box when Walker is getting a pasting from the other club.

Well, naturally, this is a most astonishing throw, indeed, but afterwards it comes out that The Sky throws a peanut loaded with lead, and of course it is not one of Harry Stevens' peanuts, either, as Harry is not selling peanuts full of lead at a dime a bag, with the price of lead what it is.

It is only a few nights after this that The Sky states another most unusual proposition to a group of citizens sitting in Mindy's restaurant when he offers to bet a C note that he can go down into Mindy's cellar and catch a live rat with his bare hands and everybody is greatly astonished when Mindy himself steps up and takes the bet, for ordinarily Mindy will not bet you a nickel he is alive.

But it seems that Mindy knows that The Sky plants a tame rate in the cellar, and this rat knows The Sky and loves him dearly, and will let him catch it any time he wishes, and it also seems that Mindy knows that one of his dish washers happens upon this rat, and not knowing it is tame, knocks it flatter than a pancake. So when The Sky goes down into the cellar and starts trying to catch a rat with his bare hands he is greatly surprised how inhospitable the rat turns out to be, because it is one of Mindy's personal rats, and Mindy is around afterwards saying he will lay plenty of 7 to 5 against even Strangler Lewis being able to catch one of his rats with his bare hands, or with boxing gloves on.

I am only telling you all this to show you what a smart guy The Sky is, and I am only sorry I do not have time to tell you about many other very remarkable propositions that he thinks up outside of his regular business.

It is well-known to one and all that he is very honest in every respect, and that he hates and despises cheaters at cards, or dice, and furthermore The Sky never wishes to play with any the best of it himself, or anyway not much. He will never take the inside of any situation, as many gamblers love to do, such as owning a gambling house, and having the percentage run for him instead of against him, for always The Sky is strictly a player, because he says he will never care to settle down in one spot long enough to become the owner of anything.

In fact, in all the years The Sky is drifting around the country, nobody ever knows him to own anything except maybe a bank roll, and when he comes to Broadway the last time, which is the time I am now speaking of, he has a hundred G's in cash money, and an extra suit of clothes, and this is all he has in the world. He never owns such a thing as a house, or an automobile, or a piece of jewellery. He never owns a watch, because The Sky says time means nothing to him.

Of course some guys will figure a hundred G's comes under the head of owning something, but as far as The Sky is concerned, money is nothing but just something for him to play with and the dollars may a well be doughnuts as far as value goes with him. The only time The Sky ever thinks of money as money is when he is broke, and the only way he can tell he is broke is when he reaches into his pocket and finds nothing there but his fingers.

Then it is necessary for The Sky to go out and dig up some fresh scratch somewhere, and when it comes to digging up scratch, The Sky is practically supernatural. He can get more potatoes on the strength of a telegram to some place or other than John D. Rockefeller can get on collateral, for everybody knows The Sky's word is as good as wheat in the bin.

Now one Sunday evening The Sky is walking along Broadway, and at the corner of Forty-ninth Street he comes upon a little bunch of mission workers who are holding a religious meeting, such as mission workers love to do of a Sunday evening, the idea being that they may round up a few sinners here and there, although personally I always claim the mission workers come out too early to catch any sinners on this part of Broadway. At such an hour the sinners are still in bed resting up from their sinning of the night before, so they will be in good shape for more sinning a little later on.

There are only four of these mission workers, and two of them are old guys, and one is an old doll, while the other is a young doll who is tootling on a cornet. And after a couple of ganders at this young doll, The Sky is a goner, for this is one of the most beautiful young dolls anybody ever sees on Broadway, and especially as a mission worker. Her name is Miss Sarah Brown.

She is tall, and thin, and has a first-class shape, and her hair is a light brown, going on blonde, and her eyes are like I do not know what, except that they are one-hundred-per-cent eyes in every respect. Furthermore, she is not a bad cornet player, if you

12

like cornet players, although at this spot on Broadway she has to play against a scat band in a chop-suey joint near by, and this is tough competition, although at that many citizens believe Miss Sarah Brown will win by a large score if she only gets a little more support from one of the old guys with her who has a big brass drum, but does not pound it hearty enough.

Well, The Sky stands there listening to Miss Sarah Brown tootling on the cornet for quite a spell, and then he hears her make a speech in which she puts the blast on sin very good, and boosts religion quite some, and says if there are any souls around that need saving the owners of same may step forward at once. But no one steps forward, so The Sky comes over to Mindy's restaurant where many citizens are congregated, and starts telling us about Miss Sarah Brown. But of course we already know about Miss Sarah Brown, because she is so beautiful, and so good.

Furthermore, everybody feels somewhat sorry for Miss Sarah Brown, for while she is always tootling the cornet, and making speeches, and looking to save any souls that need saving, she never seems to find any souls to save, or at least her bunch of mission workers never gets any bigger. In fact, it gets smaller, as she starts out with a guy who plays a very fair sort of trombone, but this guy takes it on the lam one night with the trombone, which one and all consider a dirty trick.

Now from this time on, The Sky does not take any interest in anything but Miss Sarah Brown, and any night she is out on the corner with the other mission workers, you will see The Sky standing around looking at her, and naturally after a few weeks of this, Miss Sarah Brown must know The Sky is looking at her, or she is dumber than seems possible. And nobody ever figures Miss Sarah Brown dumb, as she is always on her toes, and seems plenty able to take care of herself, even on Broadway.

Sometimes after the street meeting is over, The

Marlon Brando as
Sky and
Jean Simmons as
Sarah in the
1955 film version

SG-7400-89

13

Sky follows the mission workers to their head-quarters in an old storeroom around in Forty-eighth Street where they generally hold an indoor session, and I hear The Sky drops many a large coarse note in the collection box while looking at Miss Sarah Brown, and there is no doubt these notes come in handy around the mission, as I hear business is by no means so good there.

It is called the Save-a-Soul Mission, and it is run mainly by Miss Sarah Brown's grandfather, an old guy with whiskers, by the name of Arvide Abernathy, but Miss Sarah Brown seems to do most of the work, including tootling the cornet, and visiting the poor people around and about, and all this and that, and many citizens claim it is a great shame that such a beautiful doll is wasting her time being good.

How The Sky ever becomes acquainted with Miss Sarah Brown is a very great mystery, but the next thing anybody knows, he is saying hello to her, and she is smiling at him out of her one-hundred-per-cent eyes, and one evening when I happen to be with The Sky we run into her walking along Forty-ninth Street, and The Sky hauls off and stops her, and says it is a nice evening, which it is, at that. Then The Sky says to Miss Sarah Brown like this:

'Well,' The Sky says, 'how is the mission dodge going these days? Are you saving any souls?' he says.

Well, it seems from what Miss Sarah Brown says the soul-saving is very slow, indeed, these days.

'In fact,' Miss Sarah Brown says, 'I worry greatly about how few souls we seem to save. Sometimes I wonder if we are lacking in grace.'

She goes on up the street, and The Sky stands looking after her, and he says to me like this:

'I wish I can think of some way to help this little doll,' he says, 'especially,' he says, 'in saving a few souls to build up her mob at the mission. I must speak to her again, and see if I can figure something out.'

But The Sky does not get to speak to Miss Sarah Brown again, because somebody weighs in the sacks on him by telling her he is nothing but a professional gambler, and that he is a very undesirable character, and that his only interest in hanging around the mission is because she is a good-looking doll. So all of a sudden Miss Sarah Brown plays a plenty of chill for The Sky. Furthermore, she sends him word that she does not care to accept any more of his potatoes in the collection box, because his potatoes are nothing but ill-gotten gains.

Well, naturally, this hurts The Sky's feelings no little, so he quits standing around looking at Miss Sarah Brown, and going to the mission, and takes to mingling with the citizens in Mindy's, and showing some interest in the affairs of the community, especially the crap games.

Of course the crap games that are going on at this

time are nothing much, because practically everybody in the world is broke, but there is a head-and-head game run by Nathan Detroit over a garage in Fifty-second Street where there is occasionally some action, and who shows up at this crap game early one evening but The Sky, although it seems he shows up there more to find company than anything else.

In fact, he only stands around watching the play, and talking with other guys who are also standing around and watching, and many of these guys are very high shots during the gold rush, although most of them are now as clean as a jaybird, and maybe cleaner. One of these guys is a guy by the name of Brandy Bottle Bates, who is known from coast to coast as a high player when he has anything to play with, and who is called Brandy Bottle Bates because it seems that years ago he is a great hand for belting a brandy bottle around.

This Brandy Bottle Bates is a big, black-looking guy, with a large beezer, and a head shaped like a pear, and he is considered a very immoral and wicked character, but he is a pretty slick gambler, and a fast man with a dollar when he is in the money.

Well, finally The Sky asks Brandy Bottle why he is not playing and Brandy laughs, and states as follows:

'Why,' he says, 'in the first place I have no potatoes, and in the second place I doubt if it will do me much good if I do have any potatoes the way I am going the past year. Why,' Brandy Bottle says, 'I cannot win a bet to save my soul.'

Now this crack seems to give The Sky an idea, as he stands looking at Brandy Bottle very strangely, and while he is looking, Big Nig, the crap shooter, picks up the dice and hits three times hand-running, bing, bing, bing. Then Big Nig comes out on a six and Brandy Bottle Bates speaks as follows:

'You see how my luck is,' he says. 'Here is Big Nig hotter than a stove, and here I am without a bob to follow him with, especially,' Brandy says, 'when he is looking for nothing but a six. Why,' he says, 'Nig can make sixes all night when he is hot. If he does not make this six, the way he is, I will be willing to turn square and quit gambling forever.'

'Well, Brandy,' The Sky says, 'I will make you a proposition. I will lay you a G note Big Nig does not get his six. I will lay you a G note against nothing but your soul,' he says. 'I mean if Big Nig does not get his six, you are to turn square and join Miss Sarah Brown's mission for six months.'

'Bet!' Brandy Bottle Bates says right away, meaning the proposition is on, although the chances are he does not quite understand the proposition. All Brandy understands is The Sky wishes to wager that Big Nig does not make his six, and Brandy Bottle Bates will be willing to bet his soul a couple of times. over on Big Nig making his six, and figure he is getting the best of it, at that, as Brandy has great confidence in Nig.

Well, sure enough, Big Nig makes the six, so The Sky weeds Brandy Bottle Bates a G note, although everybody around is saying The Sky makes a terrible over-lay of the natural price in giving Brandy Bottle a G against his soul. Furthermore, everybody around figures the chances are The Sky only wishes to give Brandy an opportunity to get in action, and nobody figures The Sky is on the level about trying to win Brandy Bottle Bates' soul, especially as The Sky does not seem to wish to go any further after paying the bet.

He only stands there looking on and seeming somewhat depressed as Brandy Bottle goes into action on his own account with the G note, fading other guys around the table with cash money. But Brandy Bottle Bates seems to figure what is in The Sky's mind pretty well, because Brandy Bottle is a crafty old guy.

It finally comes his turn to handle the dice, and he hits a couple of times, and then he comes out on a four, and anybody will tell you that a four is a very tough point to make, even with a lead pencil. Then Brandy Bottle turns to The Sky and speaks to him as follows:

'Well, Sky,' he says, 'I will take the odds off you on this one. I know you do not want my dough,' he says. 'I know you only want my soul for Miss Sarah Brown, and,' he says, 'without wishing to be fresh about it, I know why you want it for her. I am young once myself,' Brandy Bottle says. 'And you know if I lose to you, I will be over there in Forty-eighth Street in an hour pounding on the door, for Brandy always settles.

'But, Sky,' he says, 'now I am in the money, and my price goes up. Will you lay me ten G's against my soul I do not make this four?'

'Bet!' The Sky says, and right away Brandy Bottle hits with a four.

Well, when word goes around that The Sky is up at Nathan Detroit's crap game trying to win Brandy Bottle Bates' soul for Miss Sarah Brown, the excitement is practically intense. Somebody telephones Mindy's where a large number of citizens are sitting around arguing about this and that, and telling one another how much they will bet in support of their arguments, if only they have something to bet, and Mindy himself is almost killed in the rush for the door.

One of the first guys out of Mindy's and up to the crap game is Regret, the horse player, and as he comes in Brandy Bottle is looking for a nine, and The Sky is laying him twelve G's against his soul that he does not make this nine, for it seems Brandy Bottle's soul keeps getting more and more expensive.

Well, Regret wishes to bet his soul against a G that Brandy Bottle gets his nine, and is greatly insulted when The Sky cannot figure his price any better than a double saw, but finally Regret accepts this price, and Brandy Bottle hits again.

Now many other citizens request a little action from The Sky, and if there is one thing The Sky cannot deny a citizen it is action, so he says he will lay them according to how he figures their word to join Miss Sarah Brown's mission if Brandy Bottle misses out, but about this time The Sky finds he has no more potatoes on him, being now around thirty-five G's loser, and he wishes to give markers.

But Brandy Bottle says that while ordinarily he will be pleased to extend The Sky this accommodation, he does not care to accept markers against his soul, so then The Sky has to leave the joint and go over to his hotel two or three blocks away, and get the night clerk to open his damper so The Sky can get the rest of his bank roll. In the meantime the crap game continues at Nathan Detroit's among the small operators, while the other citizens stand around and say that while they hear of many a daffy proposition in their time, this is the daffiest that ever comes to their attention, although Big Nig claims he hears of a daffier one, but cannot think what it is.

Big Nig claims that all gamblers are daffy anyway, and in fact he says if they are not daffy they will not be gamblers, and while he is arguing this matter back comes The Sky with fresh scratch, and Brandy Bottle Bates takes up where he leaves off, although Brandy says he is accepting the worst of it, as the dice have a chance to cool off.

Now the upshot of the whole business is that Brandy Bottle hits thirteen licks in a row, and the last lick he makes is on a ten, and it is for twenty G's against his soul, with about a dozen other citizens getting anywhere from one to five C's against their souls, and complaining bitterly of the price.

And as Brandy Bottle makes his ten, I happen to look at The Sky and I see him watching Brandy with a very peculiar expression on his face, and furthermore I see The Sky's right hand creeping inside his coat where I know he always packs a Betsy in a shoulder holster, so I can see something is wrong somewhere.

But before I can figure out what it is, there is quite a fuss at the door, and loud talking, and a doll's voice, and all of a sudden in bobs nobody else but Miss Sarah Brown. It is plain to be seen that she is all steamed up about something.

She marches right up to the crap table where Brandy Bottle Bates and The Sky and the other citizens are standing, and one and all are feeling sorry for Dobber, the doorman, thinking of what Nathan Detroit is bound to say to him for letting her in. The dice are still lying on the table showing

Brandy Bottle Bates' last throw, which cleans The Sky and gives many citizens the first means they enjoy in several months.

Well, Miss Sarah Brown looks at The Sky, and The Sky looks at Miss Sarah Brown, and Miss Sarah Brown looks at the citizens around and about, and one and all are somewhat dumbfounded, and nobody seems to be able to think of much to say, although The Sky finally speaks up as follows:

'Good evening,' The Sky says. 'It is a nice evening,' he says. 'I am trying to win a few souls for you around here, but,' he says, 'I seem to be about half out of luck.'

'Well,' Miss Sarah Brown says, looking at The Sky most severely out of her hundred-per-cent eyes, 'you are taking too much upon yourself. I can win any souls I need myself. You better be thinking of your own soul. By the way,' she says, 'are you risking your own soul, or just your money?'

Well, of course up to this time The Sky is not risking anything but his potatoes, so he only shakes his head to Miss Sarah Brown's question, and looks somewhat disorganized.

'I know something about gambling,' Miss Sarah Brown says, 'especially about crap games. I ought to,' she says. 'It ruins my poor papa and my brother Joe. If you wish to gamble for souls, Mister Sky, gamble for your own soul.'

Now Miss Sarah Brown opens a small black leather pocketbook she is carrying in one hand, and pulls out a two-dollar bill, and it is such a two-dollar bill as seems to have seen much service in its time, and holding up this deuce, Miss Sarah Brown speaks as follows:

'I will gamble with you, Mister Sky,' she says. 'I will gamble with you,' she says, 'on the same terms you gamble with these parties here. This two dollars against your soul, Mister Sky. It is all I have, but,' she says, 'it is more than your soul is worth.'

Well, of course anybody can see that Miss Sarah Brown is doing this because she is very angry, and wishes to make The Sky look small, but right away The Sky's duke comes from inside his coat, and he picks up the dice and hands them to her and speaks as follows:

'Roll them,' The Sky says, and Miss Sarah Brown snatches the dice out of his hand and gives them a quick sling on the table in such a way that anybody can see she is not a professional crap shooter, and not even an amateur crap shooter, for all amateur crap shooters first breathe on the dice, and rattle them good, and make remarks to them, such as 'Come on, baby!'

In fact, there is some criticism of Miss Sarah Brown afterwards on account of her haste, as many citizens are eager to string with her to hit, while others are just as anxious to bet she misses, and she does not give them a chance to get down.

Well, Scranton Slim is the stick guy, and he takes a gander at the dice as they hit up against the side of the table and bounce back, and then Slim hollers, 'Winner, winner, winner,' as stick guys love to do, and what is showing on the dice as big as life, but a six and a five, which makes eleven, no matter how you figure, so The Sky's soul belongs to Miss Sarah Brown.

She turns at once and pushes through the citizens around the table without even waiting to pick up the deuce she lays down when she grabs the dice. Afterwards a most obnoxious character by the name of Red Nose Regan tries to claim the deuce as a sleeper and get the heave-o from Nathan Detroit, who becomes very indignant about this, stating that Red Nose is trying to give his joint a wrong rap.

Naturally, The Sky follows Miss Brown, and Dobber, the doorman, tells me that as they are waiting for him to unlock the door and let them out, Miss Sarah Brown turns on The Sky and speaks to him as follows:

'You are a fool,' Miss Sarah Brown says.

Well, at this Dobber figures The Sky is bound to let one go, as this seems to be most insulting language, but instead of letting one go, The Sky only smiles at Miss Sarah Brown and says to her like this:

'Why,' The Sky says, 'Paul says "If any man among you seemeth to be wise in this world, let him become a fool, that he may be wise." I love you, Miss Sarah Brown,' The Sky says.

Well, now, Dobber has a pretty fair sort of memory, and he says that Miss Sarah Brown tells The Sky that since he seems to know so much about the Bible, maybe he remembers the second verse of the Song of Solomon, but the chances are Dobber muffs the number of the verse, because I look the matter up in one of these Gideon Bibles, and the verse seems a little too much for Miss Sarah Brown, although of course you never can tell.

Anyway, this is about all there is to the story, except that Brandy Bottle Bates slides out during the confusion so quietly even Dobber scarcely remembers letting him out, and he takes most of The Sky's potatoes with him, but he soon gets batted in against the faro bank out in Chicago, and the last anybody hears of him he gets religion all over again, and is preaching out in San Jose, so The Sky always claims he beats Brandy for his soul, at that.

I see The Sky the other night at Forty-ninth Street and Broadway, and he is with quite a raft of mission workers, including Mrs. Sky, for it seems that the soul-saving business picks up wonderfully, and The Sky is giving a big bass drum such a first-class whacking that the scat band in the chop-suey joint can scarcely be heard. Furthermore, The Sky is hollering between whacks, and I never see a guy look happier, especially when Mrs. Sky smiles at him out of her hundred-per-cent eyes. But I do not linger long, because The Sky gets a gander at me, and right away he begins hollering:

'I see before me a sinner of the deepest dye,' he hollers. 'Oh, sinner, repent before it is too late. Join with us, sinner,' he hollers, 'and let us save your soul.'

Naturally, this crack about me being a sinner embarrasses me no little, as it is by no means true, and it is a good thing for The Sky there is no copper in me, or I will go to Mrs. Sky, who is always bragging about how she wins The Sky's soul by outplaying him at his own game, and tell her the truth.

And the truth is that the dice with which she wins The Sky's soul, and which are the same dice with which Brandy Bottle Bates wins all his potatoes, are strictly phony, and that she gets into Nathan Detroit's just in time to keep The Sky from killing old Brandy Bottle.

Bob Hoskins as Nathan and Ian Charleson as Sky in the National Theatre production, 1982.

FRANK LOESSER

By Caryl Brahms & Ned Sherrin

I t seems to have come as a surprise to many people to learn that Frank Loesser's *Guys and Dolls* at the National Theatre is the masterpiece it has always been. Camels have had an easier job getting through the eye of a needle than eager playgoers seeking access to the Olivier auditorium.

Frank Loesser was born in 1910, twenty-two years after Irving Berlin, the other master of music who was equally at home on Broadway and down Tin Pan Alley; but Loesser died in 1969. Berlin was then a vigorous eighty year old and happily the older gentleman is still with us.

Like Berlin, Loesser was weaned on Tin Pan Alley, but again, like Berlin, he discovered that he could write songs for the theatre which sat sunnily on the stage. Indeed, in his handful of shows he was ambitious to stretch and challenge the form of the musical with an instinct for innovation which out-stripped Berlin.

He came from a family of serious musicians; his father was a piano teacher and his older brother, Arthur Loesser, an accomplished pianist and a music critic.

His first song was written at the age of six, the lyric, 'The May Party', celebrated the children's processions he watched in Central Park. At seven he listened to the clinking rhythm of the Elevated running through his neighbourhood and put words to it. He ignored his family's encouragement and trained himself, improvising on the piano, composing on the harmonica, and winning third prize in an harmonica contest. His father disapproved of popular songs.

He dropped out of City College after one year. He explained his rejection of a formal musical education by saying, 'I wasn't in the mood to learn.' However, Cynthia Lindsay in her introduction to the *Frank Loesser Song Book* points out his extraordinary versatility:

He once constructed, with great craftsmanship, the corner (just the corner) of a Regency desk, inlaid and perfectly finished. He then sent it to John Steinbeck, a piece of notepaper attached, with the printed words, 'FROM THE DESK OF FRANK LOESSER'

His first job was working with words. At eighteen he was briefly employed in New Rochelle, New York, as City Editor on the local newspaper. However, he packed a crash course in song-writing into the early years of the Thirties by using his days off to write acts for Vaudevillians. Later, he left an account of this period. 'Somehow you had to find a way of getting a job . . . The Depression was here and I even got one job checking the food and service in a string of restaurants. I was paid seventy-five cents each meal to eat eight or ten meals a day. At least I was eating, which a lot of people weren't. You had to keep alert all the time. I suppose that's where this tremendous energy of mine originated.' Energy he had, explosive energy.

He needed it to cover the range of other jobs he tried in the early 30s, working as a process server, a jewellery salesman, a waiter in a Catskill's hotel, and a press agent; and then finally getting a contract to write lyrics for the Leo Fiest music company.

He also landed a job playing and singing at The Back Drop, a night club on 52nd Street, echoed in *Guys and Dolls* as 'The Hot Box'. Finally, he placed five songs in a Broadway revue *The Illustrator's Show*, in 1936, albeit a fiasco. After the show closed, Loesser set off for California and a brief contract with Universal Pictures. It is here that history begins to record Mr. Loesser's eruptions.

Frank Loesser

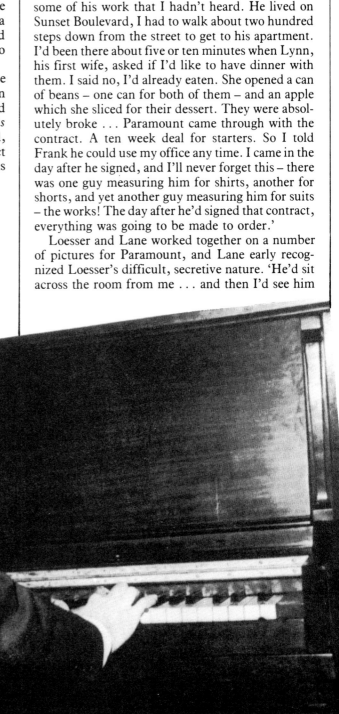

The composer, Burton Lane, observed his arrival on the Hollywood scene at a time when musicals were fashionable and, in Hoagy Carmichael's words, 'Everybody was eatin' high on the hog.' Lane was immediately impressed by Loesser's lyrics and arranged for Paramount to give him a contract. In an interview with Max Wilk, Lane vividly evokes the suspense, 'Whilst they were making up their corporate mind whether to sign him on, I had a call from Frank . . . could I come over, he wanted to show me some of his work that I hadn't heard. He lived on Sunset Boulevard, I had to walk about two hundred steps down from the street to get to his apartment. I'd been there about five or ten minutes when Lynn, his first wife, asked if I'd like to have dinner with them. I said no, I'd already eaten. She opened a can of beans – one can for both of them – and an apple which she sliced for their dessert. They were absolutely broke . . . Paramount came through with the contract. A ten week deal for starters. So I told Frank he could use my office any time. I came in the day after he signed, and I'll never forget this – there was one guy measuring him for shirts, another for shorts, and yet another guy measuring him for suits – the works! The day after he'd signed that contract, everything was going to be made to order.'

Loesser and Lane worked together on a number of pictures for Paramount, and Lane early recognized Loesser's difficult, secretive nature. 'He'd sit across the room from me . . . and then I'd see him smile . . . and suddenly he'd jump up and he had it all written out, a complete lyric. I'd put it on my piano and he'd want me to sing it right away. Hell, I hadn't even seen the lyric yet! And if I'd stumble, he'd yell, "God damn it, can't you *read*?"'

Hoagy Carmichael remembered Loesser as 'a confident little character swinging his coat-tails and whistling', glimpsed through the window of an office at Paramount. 'I never saw anybody so self assured.' Loesser was on one of his dozen or so safaris to the commissary for the constant cups of coffee with which he moistened his dogged, lonely, tormented search for appropriate words. 'At first the kid shook me up – his exuberance and zany talk were too much for me.' Carmichael felt that Loesser was insufficiently serious about his craft. He soon found that this indifference was a front. 'He'd only been joking with me to keep me happy and alive.' Their first song was 'Heart and Soul' which was used in a picture. Then, '. . . Frank said he wanted to write a song called "Small Fry". I said, "sure", and we did.'

Meanwhile, Loesser was unloading his ideas on a variety of composers.

Cy Feuer and Ernest H. Martin,
the original
producers

At Republic Pictures, a considerably less fashionable outfit than Paramount, the music department was run by Cy Feuer, who was later, with Ernest Martin, to produce *Guys and Dolls*, Loesser's biggest success. In 1941, Feuer engaged an all round musician, vocal coach, rehearsal pianist, choral director and utility conductor, Jule Styne, to do whatever chores were required around the studio. Occasionally, he wrote songs. It was a long time before Jule Styne was to write *Gentlemen Prefer Blondes*, *Funny Girl* or *Gypsy*. His unsubtle first attempt was called 'I Love Watermelon'. 'The man is eating watermelon', explained the Director. 'That's what the song has to be about. When a man is sewing a boot and singing, I want him to sing about sewing a boot.' Some months later Republic Pictures grew more ambitious. They were considering investing the, for them, huge sum of half a million dollars in a musical called *Sis Hopkins*. Styne was required to write seven songs. He asked for a good lyric writer – specifically he wanted Frank Loesser who was being paid two hundred and fifty dollars a week at Paramount. However, his loan out rate was five hundred. A compromise, which involved trading John Wayne, a Republic star to Universal for a film, was reached, and everyone was happy except the explosive Loesser. First he windmilled into Cy Feuer's office, yelling, according to Jule Styne's biographer, 'You son of a bitch, I'm writing for Hoagy Carmichael now. I'm not coming to work with some half-ass piano player who is really a vocal coach.' After two hours of persuasion by Feuer, Loesser agreed at least to talk to Styne. He had not yet agreed to work with him. Feuer recalls that when Loesser was really angry both feet had a tendency to leave the ground. Certainly neither touched the floor when he arrived at Styne's bungalow. The account comes from Theodore Taylor's biography of Styne. 'You have demeaned me by asking for me . . .', he shouted, 'you have no respect for my talent, not that I can't understand why you'd want me. But Jesus Christ, every big picture at Paramount they've been giving to Johnny Mercer. Now Goddamit, who writes the hits? Me!' Apart from 'Small Fry' and 'Two Sleepy People', they already included 'I've Got Spurs That Jingle, Jangle, Jingle' and 'Snug as a Bug in a Rug'. Then there were 'Sand In My Shoes' and 'Kiss The Boy's Goodbye', written with Victor Schertzinger.

Uncharacteristically, Jule Styne sat silent through Loesser's verbal lashing. Loesser slugged on, 'Now this pile of shit, Republic', he continued, 'you've destroyed me forever.' The fists pounded Styne's desk. 'I'm going to write these f . . . . . g songs in four days; but you're not going to hand them in for three weeks. I'm going to Palm Springs and sit on my butt. You understand that?' Abruptly, Loesser asked Styne to play him something. Styne, at last able to get a word in explained that he had requested Loesser because he wanted to write something good. He began to put his heart on his sleeve. 'I've watched horses shimmy in sync. I've written arrangements for coyotes, I've written songs about watermelon and guts and gravy . . .' Loesser's characteristic menacing pace around the confined space persisted and he silenced Styne savagely, 'I don't want your history. I hate your guts.' Styne started to play a tune and Loesser's immediate response was to stop pacing, rush to the door and slam it shut. 'Never play that song here again', he shouted, and then, modulating to a conspiratorial whisper, 'Don't ever play that song for anyone else. We'll write that song at Paramount.' 'He was that kind of schemer', Styne commented in another interview.

Hating the ambience of Republic, Loesser nonetheless worked out his time there, covering the bungalow office in which they worked with signs reading 'No Cowboys Allowed, No Horses Allowed, No Gunshots.' He did not go to Palm Springs or sit on his butt. He continued to fight with Feuer and even more fiercely with the director of the film; but Styne got used to his highly individual working methods; the tiny figure pacing and pacing the small bungalow; listening and listening to a tune over and over again. Never confiding a lyrical idea until it was fully formed in his mind. As soon as *Sis Hopkins* was finished, he arranged for Styne to be lent to Universal for *Sweater Girl*, and Styne crossed the border without declaring the tune that had so appealed to Loesser. Loesser took five weeks of anxious perambulation, smiling mysteriously to himself, drinking from his bottomless well of coffee and smoking endless cigarettes while Styne played the song again and again. At last, with no warning, Loesser arrived one morning and said that he was ready to reveal the lyric – it was 'I Don't Want to Walk Without You, Baby'.

During his first stay in Hollywood, Loesser was also to write with Arthur Schwartz, Jimmy McHugh and Frederick Hollander. With Schwartz he wrote, 'They're Either Too Young or Too Old' for Bette Davis. With Frederick Hollander he wrote the score for *Destry Rides Again*, including Dietrich's 'See What the Boys in the Back Room Will Have'.

Loesser left Hollywood for the Army with a characteristic gesture. When Jule Styne asked with whom he should now collaborate Loesser had no hesitation in saying, 'You've been spoiled. There's no one like me ... I'll tell you what. If you want someone like me, don't get a clever rhymer, because there is a thing called a rhyming dictionary. Anybody can rhyme, you can find a rhyme for anything. But get a guy who can say something clever and warm, because you need warm lyrics for your music.'

'Warm and clever' is an apt summing up of Loesser's distinctive skill, never better realized than in 'Spring Will Be A Little Late This Year'.

In the forties, Loesser wrote a series of Army songs. 'Praise the Lord and Pass the Ammunition' and 'What Do You Do In The Infantry?' among them.

The war in one of its more useful side effects subtly pushed Loesser further along the songwriter's road. For a long time the abrasive little man had been ambitious to write his own music. 'Praise the Lord and Pass the Ammunition' was the first song for which he wrote words and music and it gave him confidence to experiment further. Loesser's war songs represent the Tin Pan Alley side of his talent; but now it was time for him to start to show his Broadway paces. His first attempt was modest; but fresh and engaging. Feuer and Martin were trying to make their own Broadway debut as producers. Their project was a musical version of the old English farce, *Charley's Aunt*; the new title was *Where's Charley?*

Feuer's first instinct was to team Loesser with Harold Arlen, but when Arlen proved unavailable he and his partner decided to risk Loesser alone. There were a number of other people who had to be convinced. First there was the star, Ray Bolger, but Loesser charmed him. Then there were backers to be impressed. Rodgers and Hammerstein, who were familiar with Loesser's music, invested in the show.

In 1948 there was no more potent lure to persuade speculators to throw their money away than to give them a chance to follow Rodgers and Hammerstein up any garden path. George Abbott directed and made a charming leisurely adaptation of the play. Georges Balanchine did the choreography; but it is the range and freshness of Loesser's work which still stands out. He contributed love songs like, 'Once In Love With Amy' and 'My Darling, My Darling', which were very successful, but perhaps the song that points most directly to the innovative qualities for which Loesser's scores were to become famous is the March 'The New Ashmolean Marching Society and Student's Conservatory Band'; it embodies all his relish for setting an amusingly convoluted phrase happily on an irresistible tune as he was later to do with 'some irresponsible dress manufacturer' in *How To Succeed* and 'The Oldest Established Floating Crap Game' in *Guys and Dolls*.

Strangely, the show was slow to catch on despite congratulatory telegrams from Rodgers and Hammerstein, Cole Porter and countless other composers. Finally, Arthur Schwartz wrote an unsolicited article in the New York Times, stating quite directly that Frank Loesser was, 'the greatest undiscovered composer in America'. It tipped the balance at the box office.

Loesser's next show with Feuer and Martin was *Guys and Dolls*. This time he was teamed with Abe Burrows (after an abortive book by Jo Swerling) and the director, George S. Kaufman. He had found the perfect subject, the Broadway world of Damon Runyon and in particular 'The Idyll of Miss Sarah Brown', Loesser's essence was urban.

Max Wilk quotes Ernest Martin, 'strictly a city boy'. Loved to quote Nunnally Johnson, who said that if he had a place with green grass he'd pave it. Martin has also described Loesser's working habits at this period; they were eccentric to say the least. He rose at around four-thirty or five and made himself a martini. He was not a lush, it simply got him going. He would write from five to eight and then go back to sleep. The stint of sleep would be followed by another three or four hour burst of work and another nap. Friends whom he knew were early risers were liable to get six o'clock telephone calls to be treated to his latest work – to paraphrase his lyric, his time of day was the dark time, a couple of bars before dawn. He never agreed formally to write *Guys and Dolls*; the day he handed Feuer and Martin the first four songs was the day they knew they had a show. His eccentricities were Runyonesque. He had a phobia about sitting in public places unless his back was to the wall, and the result of teaming him with Runyon was a perfect marriage.

It was Loesser who threw out Swerling's original book; but perversely he still wrote his score around

Abe Burrows

26

it. However, his sure theatrical instinct developed so rapidly that Burrows found it possible to construct his new story line writing from song to song. 'I had those songs of Frank's to go by', Burrows told Max Wilk, 'but then we'd sit and we'd look hard for song-spots.' An exception was 'The Fugue for Tin Horns', which seemed to have no place in the plot and so was placed at the opening of the show, wonderfully setting the mood for the play and the exotic world and picturesque vocabulary of the Runyon characters who inhabited it.

Guys and Dolls not only confirmed Loesser's reputation as a song writer, but also as a volatile colleague. One of his most towering displays of temper came during the first stage rehearsal of The Crap Game number which was interpolated into the show in Philadelphia. Michael Kidd, the choreographer, was starting to stage it when Loesser launched himself at the stage from the back of the stalls in a flurry of four letter words. He wanted to hear the song loud and perfect every time. In his book, loud was good. Kidd's plea for patience was ignored: Martin's intervention simply increased the fury, 'You're Hitler! ... I'm the author and you're working for me!' The rehearsal came to a standstill. The cast came to attention. Motionless at the tops of their voices they bellowed the song; Feuer and Martin saw Loesser backing away up the aisle and followed

him out of the theatre where they watched him buy an ice cream and lick it contentedly all the way to his hotel. He had drawn attention to his music and was happy. He had heard it loud and he had heard it good.

On another occasion, he was rehearsing Isabel Bigley, as Sarah Brown, in a romantic song of considerable range, 'I'll Know'. So infuriated was Loesser by Miss Bigley's inability to perform the song without breaking somewhere in the middle of her register that he leapt on stage and punched her on the nose. Her flood of tears brought him to an awareness of what he had done and from that moment she had the upper hand – and an extremely expensive bracelet to decorate its wrist. The sharp,

Michael Kidd, the original choreographer

Vivian Blaine
the original Miss Adelaide

Sam Levene,
the original Nathan Detroit

funny songs, 'A Bushel and a Peck', 'Take Back Your Mink' and 'Adelaide's Lament', came quickly to Loesser, drawing on the idiom and life-style of the crooked but basically soft characters he had met in the thirties while playing piano at The Back Drop.

The romantic songs are not as vivid as the comic numbers, dear though they were to Loesser's heart; but they all comply cleverly with his dictum; character not event.

'I'm in the romance business', Loesser used to yell at Feuer and Martin during the out of town try-outs of *Guys and Dolls*. The argument centred around his wish to reprise ballads in the second act. Finally, George S. Kaufman, the director, and in this case arbitrator, quietened the composer who was yelling, 'When are they going to hear my songs? What the hell do you think I'm in this for?' by agreeing to reprise Loesser's ballads in the second act if Loesser would allow Kaufman to reprise some of the first act jokes.

Now that Loesser was winning awards his characteristic response each time was an unvarnished, 'I thought I should have won it three years ago.'

His next project was a musical based on Sydney Howard's 1924 play, *They Knew What They Wanted*. He called it *The Most Happy Fella*. This time there were to be no collaborators – he knew what he wanted – to go it alone. There were only fifteen minutes of spoken dialogue. Loesser was working towards an almost operatic form but he was careful not to say so. On one occasion he called the show 'an extended music comedy'. On another, he said, 'I may give the impression this show has operatic tendencies. If people feel that way – fine. Actually all it has is a great frequency of songs.' The arranger, Don Walker, phrased it more succinctly. 'This is a musical comedy expanded. Not an opera cut down.' Cynthia Lindsay recalls Loesser quoting George S. Kaufman, 'Of course be corny – just don't let them catch you at it.' So Loesser sneaked what was virtually an opera on to the stage and they didn't catch him at it. 'The programme simply called it a musical.'

His approach to Howard's play was direct and uncompromising. 'I figured take out all this political talk, the labor talk and the religious talk. Get rid of all that stuff and you have a love story.' In place of the material he had cut he introduced two comedy characters of his own. They provided the laughs – as 'Adelaide' and 'Nathan' had done in *Guys and Dolls*.

It took Loesser four years to write *The Most Happy Fella*. Violent depressions would be followed by bursts of enthusiasm and abundant creativity. He packed his score with more than thirty separate musical numbers. Choral passages, recitatives, arias, duets, trios, quartets; but this time the enormous range from vaudeville turns to floridly arioso

George S. Kaufman, the original director

Nathan Detroit in the Hot Box, London, 1953

Sarah and Sky in Havana.
London, 1953

Nathan sings
'Sue Me Sue Me,
Shoot Bullets Through Me'
in the London
production

operatic passages was not bound together by the
same consistent style and tone that Loesser had
found for *Guys and Dolls*.

Perhaps he was more at home in the city. Perhaps
the green grass of the Napa Valley needed to be
paved over with Broadway concrete before he could
tread the turf with complete assurance. Perhaps the
subject was too close to him and its central situation
too sentimental. Cynthia Lindsay points out that
Loesser, although a deeply sentimental person himself, detested oversentimentality onstage; he took as
his working slogan, 'the heart must bleed, not slob-
ber'. The degree to which his work matched that
motto is the degree to which *The Most Happy Fella*
succeeds.

Whatever the verdict it was a work of prodigal
richness. The conductor, Herbert Green, paints a

Miss Adelaide, with
wedding presents
meets Sky and Sarah
just back from
Havana.
London, 1953

vivid picture of Loesser in the vortex of production. 'If you knew Frank Loesser you were involved. You had no choice, because the man was a genius. Working with him was a mixture of wanting to kiss him or kill him. Professionally he was unreasonable, irascible, unfair and infuriating; socially he was gracious, thoughtful, gentle and totally enchanting – he would find the most miserable looking person at a party and go talk to him.'

The New York production of *The Most Happy Fella* ran for a year and a half; perhaps its flaws can best be summed up in one of its chorus numbers 'Abbondanza! . . . Che stravaganza'. Loesser was offering an abundance of abundance.

Stories of his tough business deals were always contrasted with 'funny stories, outrageous stories, stories of his enormous generosity . . . there were the friends who couldn't talk about him without crying, because he was so many things to so many people and special to each'. In *The Most Happy Fella* he was too generous to his audience.

In one of Frank Loesser's blocked periods during his work on *The Most Happy Fella*, Samuel Goldwyn offered him *Hans Christian Andersen*, the film, starring Danny Kaye. It was essentially a film for children; but it provided an alternative National Anthem for the Danes, 'Wonderful Copenhagen'. It is interesting that when a leaden stage version of *Hans Christian Andersen* was presented at the London Palladium it did not come to life. Had Loesser intended his score to be for the theatre, he would have written it differently. The man who could take on Tin Pan Alley and the Broadway certanly understood the difference between the two.

However, in *Greenwillow*, 1960, his next Broadway show, his theatrical instincts were not strong enough to breathe drama into the delicate, fragile folk tale. As Walter Kerr's review said, 'Folklore may be one dish that can't be cooked to order.' Neither the presence of Anthony Perkins in the cast nor a substantial advance could prolong the show's run above three months. Loesser was away in London on the closing night. His cable to the cast which replaced the usual formal notice ran, 'Oops – sorry'.

Next time, his feet were firmly back on the asphalt. *How To Succeed in Business Without Really Trying* was a satire on big corporations which provided him with an urban environment almost as mannered and much more identifiable than the Runyonesque fantasy of *Guys and Dolls*.

Rudy Vallee making his first Broadway appearance since *George White's Scandals of 1936*, inspired another of Loesser's epic rages. He did not want to perform one of his songs the way Loesser had written it. 'I am an interpreter of songs', was his point of view. Correctly, the producers stuck to the principle that the creator's instinct must be served and Loesser got his way; but not before he had fired off a telegram two pages long arguing that Feuer and Martin had betrayed him by not punching Vallee firmly on the nose. Shades of Isabel Bigley!

Throughout the show, Loesser rigorously followed his dictum, 'Remember a song is like a freight train moving across a stage. Every boxcar has a word on it. These people have to hear everything and understand it – fast, because in a minute the car will be gone and they'll never see it again. Make them listen and then lay it in their laps.' They

The crap game in the sewer. London, 1953

30

listened to *How To Succeed* for 1,416 performances on Broadway; and it joined the select band of American musicals to be awarded a Pulitzer Prize.

Loesser worked on one more musical, *Pleasures and Palaces*, which closed out of town, sunk it would appear, by its book.

He was a genuine original, and an innovator, not in the sense that he came to the musical theatre with a considered statement of what he felt it should achieve; but with a pragmatic assurance about what he could make it do for him. His business enterprises were as time consuming as his creative work. His music publishing company developed and encouraged young writers, notably Adler and Ross, who wrote *Pajama Game* and *Damn Yankees*; Meredith Willson, who wrote *The Music Man* and, in England, Peter Greenwell, the composer of *Twenty Minutes South*, *The Crooked Mile* and *The Mitford Girls*.

A strange contentious, ebullient, ambitious, gifted man – a street boy, always with a deal in his mind, a felicitous phrase in his soul and his eye on the stars; a genius entitled to his own assessment that he had it.

He died of lung cancer at the age of fifty-nine on 28 July 1969, a breathing machine on one side of him, a packet of cigarettes on the other.

The closing moments of the first London production (Coliseum, 1953)

32

DIRECTING GUYS AND DOLLS

by Richard Eyre, director of the N.T. production

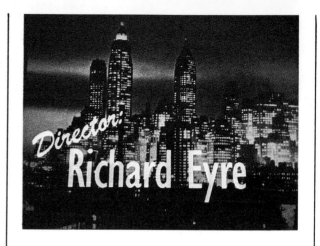

I came to *Guys and Dolls* through my father's overcoat. A loudish belted check coat with giant shoulders it was called Big Nig. 'Why,' I asked my father, at the age of 12, 'is your overcoat called Big Nig?' 'Read more than somewhat and you'll find out.' I had already read more than somewhat, in fact my eyes ached from reading by torchlight under the bedcovers. '*More Than Somewhat!*' he growled, 'by Damon Runyon!' So I read Damon Runyon and I understood. Big Nig was a crapshooter and Damon Runyon was a magical writer. About the same time (1955) the film of *Guys and Dolls* came out, a film based, according to the feed box noise, on the stories of Damon Runyon. I worshipped Brando, I adored Jean Simmons, I was cool to Sinatra, and I was entranced by the songs, and the dialogue – some of which I could even *recognize* from Runyon. In the subsequent years I came to know the original Broadway cast recording well, and had a nodding acquaintance with the script. While I was at Nottingham Playhouse I would occasionally ponder the notion of doing the show and then, daunted by the demands of the music and script, re-ponder. I never saw a stage version until my own – not even the 1979 Half Moon production, whose director told me recently that *Guys and Dolls* was so good that not even a director could mess it up . . .

Laurence Olivier planned to do *Guys and Dolls* at the National in 1970. It was cast – Olivier as Nathan, Geraldine McEwan as Adelaide, Edward Woodward as Sky and Louise Purnell as Sarah and dance rehearsals had begun. Sadly Olivier's illness nipped the production in the bud. Olivier always credited Kenneth Tynan with initiating the idea of doing *Guys and Dolls*, and my own adult enthusiasm for the show owes not a little to Tynan's advocacy. 'The second best American play' is how he described it (honours for the first going to *Death of a Salesman*).

In the middle of 1981, having been wooed by Peter Hall for some time, I agreed to join the National Theatre as an Associate Director. I had no very clear programme of plays but my first production was to be in the Olivier. Peter Hall was clearly apprehensive that I would be burning with a passion to direct a minor Ostrovsky, or exhume a Belgian masterpiece. 'Could you think,' he asked plaintively, 'of doing a major popular classic . . . ?'

A total void ensued only to be filled on a visit to a record shop specializing in Broadway Show albums and Enrico Morricone film scores by seeing the title *Guys and Dolls* on a record sleeve. That's it, I thought. In spite of the fact that I was, I discovered,

Brando and Simmons in the 1955 film

the latest in a long line of claimants to direct it at the National Peter Hall was enthusiastic. In early October it was agreed. *Guys and Dolls* to rehearse beginning of January – three months to cast, design, plan.

I had directed musicals before but never on the scale we anticipated in the Olivier; it seemed like moving from a back garden paddling pool to the Pacific Ocean. John Gunter, the designer, and I started work in mid-October. John and I have worked together intermittently for about 14 years. I suppose we operate a kind of shorthand, because in an astonishingly short time John began to develop a scheme for the show. We realized that our choices were simple: to opt for a standing set that would embrace all locations, and a production that laid little emphasis on the old fashioned production values of the Broadway musical; or to go for broke – epic, spectacular, extrovert and flamboyant: Broadway as we imagined it in its heyday. We talked a lot about films: the fluency with which Gene Kelly's films blended the conventions of studio naturalism with extreme fantasy; the affectation, parody and bravura of Scorsese's *New York, New York*; the visual hallmarks of gangster movies. We discussed each scene in terms of how we would stage it in a film version, and then translated it into the appropriate gesture for the giant jaws of the Olivier stage. We failed to persuade the National Theatre to

allow us a 'research' trip to New York. We drew very heavily on Andreas Feininger's wonderful photographs of New York in the forties. John began to create a structure that suggested Times Square by day. For night, we thought idly of neon, impractical we thought, too bright . . .

I went for a weekend in Paris and in the bookshop in the middle of the fleshless skeleton of the Beaubourg centre I encountered a book *Let There be Neon*, by Rudi Stern. I lost no time in telling John that divine intervention had occurred. The book is a loving, fastidious account of the birth, history, manufacture and current use of neon. John and I became enchanted with it – 'Neon is writing with light', Rudi Stern said, and John began to write with it. The end product, his set, is, I think, a joyous masterpiece, exploiting fully the most thrilling aspect of stage design – the ability to transform space: to move fluidly and elegantly from the epic to the intimate whilst making each location real and specific.

Sue Blane, the costume designer, provided not only marvellous costumes, but participated very actively in the frequent, long and often discursive meetings we held to plan the production with David Toguri, who was to stage the musical numbers, and with Tony Britten, the music director. What if we

Brando and Simmons in the film

did . . . ? was the constantly recurring keynote. The Havana low dive much preoccupied us. At one stage we decided to have a cafe populated entirely by émigrés from films set in Cuba–Humphrey Bogart, Lauren Bacall, Carmen Miranda, Sydney Greenstreet, Spencer Tracy, even the young Fidel Castro. We settled for a drag queen and an eccentric local clientele.

Casting went along simultaneously with planning the production. To have the talents of John Gunter, David Toguri, Sue Blane and lighting designer David Hersey was luck of a rare degree, but when it came to casting it was clear that this production had a charmed life. It is an almost invariable rule of theatre that the actor and actress you most want for a part has just signed for a film/six-part television series/two years with the RSC or emigrated. Astonishingly the people we wanted for *Guys and Dolls* were all available. It would be invidious to single out any one of the remarkably homogeneous company – each one of them not only a bright talent but possessing great generosity and wit. I have never worked with a company of such individual and collective strength. 'We want people with bumps,' said Cy Feuer of the original *Guys and Dolls* production. Our cast was richly corrugated.

All musicals are love stories – *Guys and Dolls* has two love stories, dependent on each other. It is always tempting to allow different criteria to apply to acting in musicals, to allow the artificiality of the medium to inform the performance; in short, to be untruthful. *Guys and Dolls* is a 'fairy tale of New York', peopled by many of Damon Runyan's characters but without the savage undertow of most of his stories – more Runyonesque than Runyonese, in fact. Runyon's world is a wholly successful fictional creation, as hermetic, consistent and original as Wodehouse's or Flann O'Brien's. I wanted the actors to play truthfully, without sentimentality, to present a world larger than life without parody or facetiousness. To be true, in effect, to the 'fairy tale'. Accents were studiously honed, the characters, even those on the periphery, were invested with offstage biographies. Runyon's stories were always on hand and a profesional croupier came in to teach us how to shoot craps.

We started rehearsals on 4 January 1982 – a seven week stint during which many of the cast had to learn from scratch to dance and sing harmonies, and all had to learn a tap routine. I was possessed by the idea that the show must end with the entire cast tap dancing down Broadway; it seemed to be obligatory that what was substantially an *acting* company had to dance en masse for the finale. Fortunately there was David Toguri to teach them. No choreographer I know has his skill and tact with actors, his invention and his indomitable good humour; a true alchemist.

The show rapidly began to work its magic – the songs are irresistible, the book is perfectly crafted. It is essentially a play with music – that is to say that the songs are *always* a logical extension of the dramatic situation and always impel the dramatic momentum rather than allowing it to stand still. The irony of the show's creation is that almost all the songs were written by Frank Loesser before the dialogue, which merely serves to highlight Loesser's genius as a dramatic lyricist. Abe Burrows wrote the book after an abortive script by Jo Swerling had been abandoned. 'Make it funny,' said George Kaufman, the director. 'But not *too* funny,' added Loesser. Abe Burrows certainly made it funny, but if I were looking for the catalytic talent that made *Guys and Dolls* I would lay six to five on Kaufman. A marvellous playwright (with Moss Hart and many others; he was known as 'The Great Collaborator') and play-maker (as director), George Kaufman was an exacting and utterly professional craftsman. He insisted on regarding *Guys and Dolls* as a play interrupted by musical numbers. Indeed, so strongly did he feel this that most of the songs in the show were, to Kaufman, 'lobby' numbers – every time a song started he sprinted for the lobby. Abe Burrows once overheard him, mid-sprint, mutter 'Good God, do we have to do *every* number this son-of-a-bitch ever wrote?'

Rehearsing *Guys and Dolls* was hugely demanding but pure pleasure. 'It beats working,' said Bob Hoskins to me on more than one occasion. Because the show is so well put together, there is almost a mathematical precision to it that demands that you

get it *right*. 'Musicals are not written, they're fixed' runs the adage. If you are doing a show which has been fixed to perfection, run for countless performances in countless productions you know that if something isn't working it's not the show's fault, it's yours. Ironically, this is comforting.

As the first night approached every third person I met seemed to have seen the original Broadway production, loved the film, knew every word of the lyrics, had played the parts and married one of the chorus. The stakes seemed impossibly high, gambling metaphors avalanched in the press. This was a hand we had to win gloriously or crap out in ignominy. Finally the pleasure the cast took in the show and in each other's company, the sheer volume of hard work allied to talent, communicated itself to the audience: we had a success. I even learned to tap dance.

Sinatra and Blaine in the film version

The crap game in the sewer. Brando (right) and Sinatra (centre) in the film version

THE N.T. PRODUCTION REVIEWED

by Russell Davies

Why,' ran the eternal question before this production opened, 'should our National Theatre be doing an American musical, a hit from the *commercial stage*?' Even at the time, there were ready answers to this, such as 'Why shouldn't they?' and 'In the cultural climate most of us hope for, there will scarcely be any such thing as the *un*commercial stage.' But the sight of the thing being done, on the broad apron of the Olivier, has banished theory in any case. *Guys and Dolls* is a terrific show, performed really well, and those who would rather it hadn't happened are revealed as wet blankets of the soggiest kind.

The process wouldn't have worked with any old musical. A National Theatre *Oklahoma* would necessarily have turned out as corn-fed pastiche with outbursts of lumbering 'sincerity'. But because *Guys and Dolls* is openly and proudly a low-life pastiche to begin with, it doesn't even matter that we realize the performers are not native Americans. In fact this enhances the affection in which we hold the show (which is not too stale an affection either, because there are some fine neglected numbers in the score). The first neon signs that come warmly roasting into view to establish the Manhattan landscape (settings: John Gunter, lighting: David Hersey) are 'Wrigley's Spearmint' and 'Maxwell House Coffee' – which suggest a comforting overlap of economies, if not of cultures, between ourselves and Damon Runyon's zoot-suited metropolis.

Vocally, we get the same overlap from the cast. After hard work, the accents throughout are a most honourable near-miss. Only Julia McKenzie as Miss Adelaide truly strikes the ear as a possible American import, and she has the advantage of the kind of song (a poissun can develop a cold) that practically can't be sung except in pungent Brooklynese. Bill Paterson, as Harry the Horse, has his own solution, a nasal delivery suggesting Walter Matthau in an adenoids crisis. It took time to work Harry out – a pleasant occupation even if Richard Eyre's hot-foot direction didn't leave you many spare moments in which to indulge it.

But it was the way Paterson *moved* that gave the real clue to the evening's success. This Harry the Horse doesn't walk, he treads – in a rubber-soled, bent-kneed, interior-sprung manner drawn straight from the early American comic papers and animated films. And looking around the ensemble, one realized that everybody had some speciality of this kind going for him. Larrington Walker, to take a single example, was a one-man Harlem at all times. I mean no slight on the dancing profession when I say that the one giant strength of this production was that everything was done by actors. Gone – completely gone – was any sense that a stiff-backed phalanx of principals was being eased through the strenuous part of the evening by a lithe *corps de ballet*. This is an authentic all-singing, all-dancing cast, and though everyone isn't equally good at everything, they're aiming to be, and they all count. The sense of unity achieved by David Toguri's staging was an exhilaration and a delight.

A programme note records Runyon as saying 'To Hell with plots.' People, he claimed, 'remember the characters.' This is certainly true of *Guys and Dolls*, whose plot could be comfortably inscribed on half a postage stamp. Almost its only working part is the bet contracted between Nathan Detroit and Sky Masterson, as to whether the suave, high-rolling Sky from Colorado (nice vocal distinction by Ian Charleson) will persuade Sarah the Salvation Army girl to accompany him on a binge/spree in Havana. Possibly because the process of theatre-going is in several respects emotionally akin to betting – as a show progresses one is constantly placing one's metaphorical money on the characters and shifting the investment about – the audience takes to this gladly, and requires little else in the way of propulsion through a $2\frac{3}{4}$-hour show.

But there is plenty of extra gas, and it comes direct from the music. Astonishingly – well, I wasn't aware of it – there are no weak numbers in *Guys and Dolls*. If there is a weakness in the apportioning of Frank Loesser's songs, it's that Nathan Detroit's musical share doesn't match his part in the plot; but this may have come as a relief to Bob Hoskins, whose singing isn't the best of him. Raucous even when *sotto voce*, he is very fine in the dramatic sequences, and probably the only member of the cast whose shape actually justifies a double-breasted suit. David Healy's Nicely-Nicely Johnson wears a perpetual beaming smile that isn't all the role. This is the very picture of an actor seizing, successfully, the part he was built for (come to think of it, I take it all back about Hoskins's exclusive right to The Suit).

Charleson's Sky, a Gary Cooper-style Western hero in better-draped civvies, rises to the songs with unexpected relish, and the climactic note he supplies to *Luck Be a Lady* tops off the superbly-set sewer encounter in the only appropriate way. He also blends very affectingly with Julie Covington in *I've Never Been in Love Before*, the first-half closer – and this is a stroke of luck, because Miss Covington's voice is of such a special timbre (described by a perceptive early admirer as 'like celery') that she isn't easily matched. Hers is easily the toughest role of the night: Sarah is the only character hinting at emotional depth. The plot dictates that her early entrances should put a damper on the gamblers' cavortings, which doesn't make it easier for her to establish herself; but she has nothing to worry about. The Havana scene – brilliantly stoked up by the opening solo from Bobby Orr at the drums – sets her free for what is, in the circumstances, a heroically thoughtful performance. The blend with Julia McKenzie, in their pre-closer *Marry the Man Today*, is again excellent. Miss McKenzie of course, given a whole evening's opportunity to send up her own piercingly traditional skill in the old show-stopper game, is on a winner from the start. I thought there were moments when both ladies would have been helped by some lusher musical upholstery, but the decision not to have strings was apparently forced by budgetary considerations. It did leave the orchestrations leaning sometimes a bit too close to the Brechtian wind-band tradition.

Everyone agrees that *Guys and Dolls* is a 'perfectly efficient mechanism', but there is heart in it too. The book is full of gags that work, or woik ('His wife's havin' a baby. He's noivous, it's his foist wife'), and songs that are more various, musically, than anyone has a right to expect from a single source. Justice is done to the original author's style (*Take Back Your Mink, To From Whence It Came*), and though the tale is determinedly simple-minded, the talents of our National actors are nevertheless stretched in all available directions. I don't ask for anything more, apart from the chance of buying some more tickets.

The world premiere of *Guys and Dolls* was on 24 November 1950 at the Forty-Sixth Street Theatre, New York, where it ran for 1,194 performances. Even now (1982) this makes it one of the top 50 longest running New York shows. Robert Alda played Sky, Isabel Bigley played Sarah, and Sam Levene was Nathan. Vivian Blaine was the original Adelaide but the programme above shows that Martha Stewart took over the role within the first year.

The first London production of *Guys and Dolls* opened at the Coliseum on 28 May 1953 and ran for 555 performances. The programme (above) shows that Vivian Blaine and Sam Levene of the New York cast were still Adelaide and Nathan, but Edmund Hockridge (having taken over from Jerry Wayne) and Lizbeth Webb were Sky and Sarah.

Characters in order of appearance

Benny Southstreet		**Barrie Rutter**
Nicely-Nicely Johnson		**David Healy**
Rusty Charley		**Kevin Williams**
Sarah		**Julie Covington**
Arvide Abernathy		**John Normington**
Agatha	The Mission Band	**Rachel Izen**
Calvin		**Robert Ralph**
Martha		**Belinda Sinclair**
Harry the Horse		**Bill Paterson**
Lieutenant Brannigan		**Harry Towb**
Nathan Detroit		**Bob Hoskins**
Angie the Ox	The Crap-Shooters	**Robert Oates**
Brandy Bottle Bates		**Norman Warwick**
Scranton Slim		**Richard Walsh**
Joey Perhaps		**Kevin Quarmby**
Regret		**Robert Ralph**
Society Max		**William Armstrong**
Liverlips Louis		**Larrington Walker**
Hot Horse Herbie		**Bernard Sharpe**
Sky Rocket		**Mark Bond**
Miss Adelaide		**Julia McKenzie**
Hot Box Girls		**Sally Cooper** / **Fiona Hendley**
Sky Masterson		**Ian Charleson**
Voice of Joey Biltmore		**Robert Oates**
Master of Ceremonies		**William Armstrong**
More Hot Box Girls		**Rachel Izen** / **Belinda Sinclair**
Mimi		**Imelda Staunton**
General Cartwright		**Irlin Hall**
Big Jule		**James Carter**
Drunk		**Norman Warwick**
Waiter in the Hot Box		**Kevin Williams**

The Choo-Choo Boys Band

Tony Britten (Music Director), **Terry Davies** (Assistant Music Director, keyboards), **Lennie Bush** (bass, bass guitar), **Mitch Dalton** (guitar, banjo), **Martin Drover** (trumpet), **Howard Evans** (trumpet), **Andy Findon** (flute, piccolo, saxophone), **Ian Green** (percussion), **John Harle** (clarinet, saxophone), **Paul Nieman** (trombone), **Bobby Orr** (drums), **Steve Saunders** (bass trombone), **Ray Warleigh** (saxophone, clarinet, flute), **David White** (saxophone, bass clarinet, flute)

Songs

Act One

Opening	Ensemble
Fugue for Tin Horns	Nicely-Nicely, Benny, Rusty Charley
Follow the Fold	Mission Group
The Oldest Established	Nathan, Nicely-Nicely, Benny, Ensemble
I'll Know	Sarah and Sky
A Bushel and a Peck	Adelaide and the Hot Box Girls
Adelaide's Lament	Adelaide
Guys and Dolls	Nicely-Nicely and Benny
If I Were a Bell	Sarah
My Time of Day	Sky
I've Never Been In Love Before	Sky and Sarah

Act Two

Take Back Your Mink	Adelaide and the Hot Box Girls
Reprise: Adelaide's Lament	Adelaide
More I Cannot Wish You	Arvide
Luck, Be a Lady	Sky and the Crapshooters
Sue Me	Nathan and Adelaide
Sit Down, You're Rockin' the Boat	Nicely-Nicely and Ensemble
Reprise: Follow the Fold	Mission Group
Marry the Man Today	Adelaide and Sarah
Reprise: Guys and Dolls	Entire Company

Director	**Richard Eyre**
Musical Staging	**David Toguri**
Music Arrangements	**Tony Britten & Terry Davies**
Settings	**John Gunter**
Costumes	**Sue Blane**
Lighting	**David Hersey**
Staff Director	**Kenneth Mackintosh**
Assistant Director	**Antonia Bird**
Assistant Designer	**Chris Townsend**
Dialect Coach	**Joan Washington**
Production Manager	**Michael Cass Jones**
Stage Manager	**John Rothenberg**
Deputy Stage Manager	**Angela Bissett**
Assistant Stage Managers	**Catherine Bird, Michael Roberts** **Neville Ware**
Sound Design	**Derrick Zieba** **Ric Green**
Assistant to the Lighting Designer	**Peter Radmore**
Assistant to David Toguri	**Rachel Izen**
Assistant Production Manager	**Mark Taylor**
Production photographed by **John Haynes**	

The National Theatre, London, production of *Guys and Dolls* (above) opened at the Olivier Theatre on 9 March 1982. All subsequent photos are from this production.

GUYS AND DOLLS

A musical fable of Broadway

Based on a story and characters of Damon Runyon

Music and Lyrics by Frank Loesser

Book by Jo Swerling & Abe Burrows

I

Broadway

Music: opening number – 'Runyonland'.

Discovered stage centre are two shady Broadway characters. Man with newspaper crosses from R. to L. and exit.

Bobby soxers enter L., exit R.

Sightseeing Guide and Sightseers enter L.

Actor and actress enter L. cross to L.
One of the shady Broadway characters is flipping a coin, the other snapping his fingers. They both glance offstage R. and L. obviously looking for a pickup.

A N.Y. policeman swinging a club enters from R. strolling, he exits R.

Two chorus girls wearing slacks enter from R. They exit L. Two very animated bobby soxers enter from L. carrying autograph books and pencils, they rush off R.

Two well dressed street walkers enter from R. stop at L.C. and flirt with the two shady characters, one of the shady characters flips the coin, they take two chorus girls by the arm and escort them off L.

A man rushes on from L., and exits hurriedly R.

An elderly woman street vendor dressed shabbily and carrying a shoulder tray containing apples, gardenias, and pretzels on sticks enters from L. and slowly exits stage R.

A sightseeing Texan and his wife enter from R. He is carrying a sightseeing map and wears a watch chain across his vest.

A sidewalk photographer enters from L. carrying a camera, and order blank. He snaps the Texan and his wife who pose for the photographer, photographer hands order blank to Texan who signs it and gives money to him in payment. The Texan and his wife exit L. The photographer looks after them, crumples up the order blank and throws it away.

An actress enters from R. dressed very elegantly, carrying long cigarette holder. She is escorted by an actor dressed in a tuxedo, the two bobby soxers have followed them on from R. They have the actor and actress autograph their books, as the actor and actress turn upstage to exit L., a sign painted 'Pessimo Cigars' is revealed. The bobby soxers exit R.

A man paper doll vendor and his lady assistant enter from R. pushing a trick convertible vehicle which converts into a baby buggy. They exit L.

A heavyweight prizefighter with cauliflower ears enters from R., skipping rope. His manager enters with him giving him instructions as they cross the stage and exit L.

Paper doll vendor and his assistant enter from L. with vehicle, they set it up at stage centre. Lady assistant pulls out black thread, he sets paper doll on thread, she manipulates the paper doll on the black thread, they see the policeman who enters from R. They quickly pull the trigger which converts the vehicle into a baby buggy, they nod very graciously to the policeman as they pass him, he nods, then suddenly he realizes he has been tricked, rushes off R. chasing them.

A sightseeing Guide enters from R. followed by a group of seven or eight sightseers including the Texan and his wife who are in the rear of the group. The sightseeing guide is pointing to objects of interest. A pickpocket enters from R. goes to Texan and points to a tall building and as the Texan is looking up he steals the Texan's watch and chain. The Texan and his wife exit L.

Two street walkers enter from L. They cross to the pickpocket and flirt with him and relieve him of the watch and chain he stole from the Texan. They take the pickpocket by the arm and very nonchalantly stroll off R. with him. Texan and his wife rush on from R. It is very evident that he has suddenly discovered the loss of his watch and is intent upon catching the pickpocket, they exit R.

A blind man carrying a cane, tin cup in his hand, glasses, and wearing a sign 'Blind' enters from R. He feels his way slowly to centre stage.
Paper doll vendor and his lady assistant enter from L. and set up their vehicle at stage centre, as they do so the man vendor flicks his cigarette ashes into blind man's tin cup, blind man looks at this. At this moment the paper doll vendor looks off stage R. sees policeman, motions to his assistant, picks up vehicle and rushes off L., blind man runs off L.

Pickpocket, sidewalk cameraman rush on from R. chased by the policeman, Texan and his wife, they exit L. All the characters on stage run off L. after them very excitedly.

Benny Southstreet enters from R. very engrossed in reading a racing scratch sheet.

Prizefighter, shadow boxing, enters from L. followed by his manager. The Prizefighter, not seeing Benny, runs into him accidentally. He is knocked down by the force of Benny's head against his solar plexus. Prizefighter, frightened and not knowing really what happened, runs off R. followed by his manager. Benny straightens his hat which has been dented by the collision.

Benny unconcernedly joins Nicely-Nicely Johnson, who has entered at this moment from stage L. finishing a bottle of Coca-Cola and is at the newsstand buying a scratch sheet from the newsman.

Rusty Charlie enters from L. reading a scratch sheet, they group together and sing —

FUGUE FOR TINHORNS

NICELY:
I got the horse right here
The name is Paul Revere
Two streetwalkers enter R., stand watching Benny, Nicely and Rusty.
And here's a guy that says if the weather's
  clear
Can do, can do, this guy says the horse can do
If he says the horse can do, can do, can do.
Crosses to R. passing Rusty
Can do – can do – this guy says the horse can
  do
If he says the horse can do – can do, can do.
For Paul Revere I'll bite
I hear his foot's all right
Of course it all depends if it rained last night.
Likes mud, likes mud, this 'X' means the
  horse likes mud

If that means the horse likes mud, likes mud,
  likes mud.

I tell you Paul Revere
Now this is no bum steer
It's from a handicapper that's real sincere
Can do, can do, this guy says the horse can do
If he says the horse can do – can do – can do
Paul Revere. I got the horse right here.

BENNY *Shows sheet to Rusty:*
I'm pickin' Valentine, 'cause on the morning line
The guy has got him figured at five to nine
Has chance, has chance, this guy says the horse has chance
If he says the horse has chance, has chance, has chance.

I know it's Valentine, the morning works look fine
Besides the jockey's brother's a friend of mine
Needs race, needs race, this guy says the horse needs race
If he says the horse needs race – needs race, needs race.
I go for Valentine, 'cause on the morning line
The guy has got him figured at five to nine
Has chance, has chance, this guy says the horse has chance.
Valentine! I got the horse right here.

RUSTY CHARLIE *Crosses to R. of Benny:*
But look at Epitaph. He wins it by a half,
According to this here in the Telegraph
'Big Threat' – 'Big Threat'
This guy calls the horse 'Big Threat'
If he calls the horse 'Big Threat'
Big Threat, Big Threat.

And just a minute, boys,
I got the feed box noise
Shows class, shows class,
This guy says the horse shows class
It says the great-grandfather was Equipoise
If he says the horse shows class
Shows class, shows class.
So make it Epitaph, he wins it by a half
According to this here in the Telegraph
Epitaph, I got the horse right here!

At end of 'Fugue for Tinhorns' Mission Band enters playing 'Follow the Fold', Sarah with tambourine, a female member playing the trombone, a male member playing the cornet, Arvide Abernathy beating a bass drum and cymbals, a female member is carrying a small box which she places stage C. Sarah steps on the box and as they finish playing they sing 'Follow the Fold'. Two bobby soxers enter from R. They stop and listen.

SARAH AND MISSION BAND:
Follow the fold and stray no more
Stray no more, stray no more
Put down the bottle and we'll say no more.
Drunk enters from R. steps to L. of Sarah.
Follow, follow the fold.
Sightseeing Group, including Texan and his wife enter L.

SARAH *Points at drunk:*
Before you take another swallow.
Prizefighter and his Manager enter from R. stop at centre, then move back to R. and they listen to singing.

SARAH AND BAND:
Follow the fold and stray no more
Stray no more, stray no more
Tear up your poker deck and play no more
Follow, follow the fold,
To the meadows where the sun shines.
Chorus Girls (2) enter from L. stop suddenly to L. of Sarah, alongside of the drunk, Sarah points at them.

SARAH:
Out of the darkness and the cold.
And the sin and shame in which you wallow.
She points again to Chorus Girls.

SARAH AND BAND:
Follow the fold and stray no more
Stray no more, stray no more
If you're a sinner and you pray no more
Follow, follow the fold.
At end of song Sarah immediately goes into her speech.

SARAH: Brothers and sisters, resist the Devil and he will flee from you. That is what the Bible tells us.
Nicely, Benny, Rusty cross to L.
And that is why I am standing here, in the Devil's own city,
The bobby soxers exit laughingly L.
on the Devil's own street, prepared to do battle with the forces of evil.
Hear me, you gamblers!
She points to Nicely, Benny and Rusty who are standing stage L.C., they move uneasily to stage L.

SARAH: With your dice, your cards, your horses!
Pause and think before it is too late!
She is failing to hold her audience, and occasionally falters in her speech as she notices someone walk out.
You are in great danger! I am not speaking of the prison and the gallows,
Sightseeing Group exits R.
but of the greater punishment that awaits you!
Repent before it is too late!
Prizefighter and his Manager exit L.
Just around the corner is our little Mission
Drunk exits L.

where you are always welcome to seek refuge from this jungle of sin.

Two Chorus Girls exit L.

Come there and talk to me. Do not think of me as Sergeant Sarah Brown, but as Sarah Brown, your sister.

The two street walkers slowly exit L. showing their wares as they pass Rusty Charlie, who is standing at newsstand with Nicely and Benny. He follows them off, pointing his finger at them as they exit. Nicely and Benny are not conscious of this.

Join me, Brothers and Sisters, in resisting the Devil, and we can put him to flight forever.

Sarah looks at Arvide hopelessly, he motions to her encouragingly.

Remember, friends, it is the Save-A-Soul Mission (*slowly stepping down from the box*) located at 409 West 49th Street, open all day and all night, with a special prayer meeting next Thursday at –

Looks despairingly at Arvide, her crowd has disappeared by this time, except Nicely and Benny who are standing by the newsstand reading their scratch sheets. Sarah and the Mission Band make a disconsolate and disorderly exit L.

Music as they exit.

NICELY *Looking after them as he crosses to stage C., followed by Benny:* Poor Miss Sarah! I wonder why a refined doll like her is mixed up in the Mission dodge.

BENNY: She is a beautiful doll, all right, with one hundred per cent eyes.

NICELY: It is too bad that such a doll wastes all her time being good. How can she make any money from that?

BENNY: Maybe she owns a piece of the Mission.

NICELY: Yeah.

Harry the Horse enters from L. crosses to Benny.

HARRY: Hey! Benny Southstreet! *They shake hands.*

BENNY: Harry the Horse! How are you!

HARRY: Okay, okay.

BENNY: You know Nicely-Nicely Johnson.

HARRY: Yeah. How goes it?

NICELY: Nicely, nicely, thank you.

HARRY: Tell me, what about Nathan Detroit? Has he got a place for his crap game?

BENNY *Whispers back.* We don't know yet.

NICELY: The heat is on.

BENNY: He's still trying to find a place.

HARRY: Well, tell him I'm loaded and ready for action. *Crosses to R., past Nicely.* I just acquired five thousand potatoes.

BENNY: Five thousand Dollars!

NICELY: Where did you acquire it?

HARRY: I collected the reward on my father.

Exits R.

BENNY: Everybody is looking for action. *He stops as*

Brannigan enters – gets paper at newsstand – crosses to Benny. Slowly. I hope Nathan finds a – place.

NICELY: Why, Lieutenant Brannigan! Mr. South-street, it is Lieutenant Brannigan of the New York Police Department.

BENNY *Crosses to R.* A pleasure. *Moves away.*

BRANNIGAN: Any of you guys seen Nathan Detroit? *Reading.*

BENNY: Which Nathan Detroit is that?

Brannigan folds his paper with an abrupt movement and faces the two men.

BRANNIGAN: I mean the Nathan Detroit who's been running a floating crap game around here, and getting away with it by moving it to a different spot every night.

NICELY: Why are you telling us this – Your Honour?

BRANNIGAN: I am telling you because I know you two bums work for Detroit, rustling up customers for his crap game.

NICELY: We do?

BRANNIGAN: Yeah!

NICELY: Oh!

BRANNIGAN: You can tell him from me: I know that right now he's running around trying to find a spot. Well, nobody's gonna give him a spot, because they all know that Brannigan is breathing down their neck! *Starts to exit. Turns round left. Nathan enters from above newsstand, with hat on, not seeing Brannigan.*

NATHAN: Fellers, Fellers...

NICELY: Hi, Nathan!

NATHAN: Fellows, I'm in real terrible trouble. That lousy Brannigan, and I can't –

BRANNIGAN: Something wrong, Mr. Detroit?

NATHAN *A sickly grimace:* Oh, hello, Lieutenant. I hope you don't think I was talking about you. There are other lousy Brannigans.

BRANNIGAN: Detroit, I have just been talking to your colleagues about your crap game. I imagine you are having trouble finding a place.

NATHAN: Well, the heat is on, as you must know from the fact that you now have to live on your salary.

Brannigan glares and exits L.

BENNY *Crosses to Nathan:* Did you find a place?

NATHAN: What does that cop want from me? What am I – a sex maniac? I merely run a crap game for the convenience of those who want a little action, in return for which I take a small cut. Is that a crime! *Boys shake heads.* Yeah!

BENNY: Nathan! Did you find a place?

NICELY: Did you find a place for the game?

NATHAN *Crosses to R. passes Nicely:* Did I find a place. Did I find a place! – yes, I found a place! We are holding the crap game tomorrow night on the top of Mount Everest.

NATHAN: I tried all the regular places. The back of the cigar store, the funeral parlour –

NICELY: Nathan, you said once there might be a chance for the Biltmore Garage.

NATHAN: I went to the Biltmore Garage. *Benny crosses to Nathan, Nicely follows.* – spoke to Joey Biltmore himself. He says he might take a chance and let me use the place, if I give him a thousand bucks.

BENNY: A thousand bucks!

NATHAN: In cash. *Pushes Benny.* He won't take my marker.

BENNY: Your marker's no good, huh? *Nathan crosses to stage L.*

NATHAN: What do you mean? *Pushes Benny against Nicely.* My marker is as good as cash, only Joey Biltmore wants cash ... It don't seem possible. Me without a livelihood. Why, I've been running the crap game ever since I was a juvenile delinquent. *Crosses L.C.*

BENNY *Crosses to Nathan:* Nathan, can't you do something?

NATHAN: What can I do? I'm broke. *Crosses between Benny and Nicely.* I couldn't even buy Adelaide a present today, and you know what today is? It is mine and Adelaide's fourteenth anniversary.

BENNY: Yeah?

NICELY: Yeah?

NATHAN: Yeah. We been engaged for fourteen years.

THE OLDEST ESTABLISHED

Three Crap Shooters enter from L., go to newsstand and converse.

BENNY: Nathan, concentrate on the game. The town's up to here with high players. The Greek's in town!

NICELY: Brandy Bottle Bates!
Two Crap Shooters enter from R.
BENNY: Scranton Slim!
Two Crap Shooters enter from L.
NATHAN: I know. *Steps forward.* I could make a
fortune. But where can I have the game?
NICELY *Sings:*
The Biltmore garage wants a grand.
BENNY:
But we ain't got a grand on hand.
Crosses between Nicely and Nathan
NATHAN:
And they've now got a lock on the door
Of the gym at Public School Eighty-four.
NICELY:
There's the stock-room behind McClosky's
Bar.
Crosses to Nathan
BENNY:
But Missus McClosky ain't a good scout.
NATHAN:
And things bein' *(crosses to R. past Benny)* –
how they are.
The back of the Police Station's out.
NICELY:
So the Biltmore garage is the spot.
ALL THREE:
But the one-thousand bucks we ain't got.
Three Crap Shooters enter from R.
FIRST CRAP SHOOTER:
Why it's good old reliable Nathan.
THREE CRAP SHOOTERS:
Nathan, Nathan, Nathan Detroit.
MORE CRAP SHOOTERS:
If you're looking for action he'll furnish the
spot.
Two men enter L.
STILL MORE CRAP SHOOTERS:
Even when the heat is on it's never too hot.
Three men enter R.
ALL THE CRAP SHOOTERS:
Not for good old reliable Nathan for it's always
just a short walk.
They all gather downstage.

They take off their hats.
To the oldest established permanent floating
crap game in New York.
Move to C.

There are well-heeled shooters ev'rywhere,
ev'rywhere.
There are well-heeled shooters ev'rywhere –
And an awful lot of lettuce *(shows money)*
For the fella who can get us there. *Back
upstage.*

NICELY, BENNY, NATHAN:
If we only had a lousy little grand we could be
a millionaire.

ALL:
That's – Good old reliable Nathan, Nathan,
Nathan, Nathan Detroit.

All come downstage.
If the size of your bundle you want to increase
He'll arrange that you go broke in quiet and
peace
In a hideout provided by Nathan where there
are no neighbours to squawk
(*they all stand straight*). It's the oldest
established permanent floating (*whisper*)
crap game in New York.
Where's the action? Where's the game?

NICELY, BENNY, NATHAN:
Gotta have the game or we'll die from shame.

ALL *All stand up straight:*
It's the oldest established (*take hats off*)
permanent floating crap game in New York.
*All the Crap Shooters start to exit R. and L. Nathan
shouts after them as they exit.*

NATHAN: Gentlemen, do not worry. Nathan
Detroit's crap game will float again. My boys will
let you know where it is.
They all exit R. and L.

ANGIE-THE-OX: Okay, Nathan . . . Say, you know
who else is looking for action? Sky Masterson!
Sky Masterson's in town.

Angie exits R.

NATHAN: Sky Masterson! There is the highest player of them all!

BENNY: Higher than the Greek?

NATHAN: Higher than anybody. Why do you think they call him Sky? That's how high he bets. *Crosses to centre.* I once saw him bet five thousand dollars on a Caterpillar race. And another time he was sick, and he wouldn't take penicillin on account he had bet ten G's that his temperature would go to 104.

NICELY: Did it?

NATHAN: Did it? He's so lucky it went to 106. Good old Sky.

NICELY: Maybe you can borrow the thousand from Sky.

NATHAN: No. Not Sky. With him that kind of money ain't lending money – *Crosses to R.* It's betting money. So why don't I bet him? Why don't I bet him a thousand on something?

NICELY: You would bet with Sky Masterson?

NATHAN *Crosses between Benny and Nicely and places his hands on their shoulders.* I ain't scared. I am perfectly willing to take the risk, providing I can figure out a bet on which I know I cannot lose. He likes crazy bets, like which lump of sugar will a fly sit on; or how far can you kick a piece of cheesecake. Cheesecake! Benny! Look – run into Mindy's Restaurant and ask Mindy how many pieces of cheesecake he sold yesterday and also how many pieces of strudel.

BENNY: How much cheesecake, how much strudel – What do you want to know for?

NATHAN: Just find out! Oi! Here comes Adelaide. *Crosses to L. of Benny as he looks off L.* If she hears I am running the crap game she will never set foot on me again. Go on, beat it. *Moves back to centre. Benny and Nicely run off R. as Adelaide enters L. carrying a small box which contains a man's belt and a small card. She is followed by three girls from the Hot Box.*

NATHAN: Adelaide! Pigeon!

ADELAIDE: Nathan. Darling! *Embrace.* The three girls have stopped at stage R. on the greetings.

ADELAIDE *Crosses to three girls.* Oh, girls, you go on ahead, I'll see you later.

GIRLS: Okay, Adelaide – *They exit R.*

ADELAIDE: We gotta get right back to the Hot Box in ten minutes.

NATHAN: You still rehearsing?

ADELAIDE *Crosses back to Nathan.* Yeah. It's that slave driver Charlie – he's been working us all day. Finally I says, 'Look, Charlie, I'm starving! I gotta get outa here and get something to eat.' And he says, 'You don't want to eat. You just want to

sneak out and meet that cheap bum, Nathan Detroit!'...

NATHAN *Outraged.* So what did you tell him?

ADELAIDE *Proudly:* I told him. *To Nathan.* I says 'I'll meet whoever I want!'...

NATHAN: Well, don't upset yourself. How's your cold?

ADELAIDE: Oh, it's much better thank you ... *Steps back.* Nathan! Happy Anniversary!

NATHAN: A present! For me?

ADELAIDE: I hope you like it.

NATHAN: A belt!

ADELAIDE: Read the card!

NATHAN: 'Sugar is sweet and so is jelly, so put this belt around your belly.' Darling, that's so sweet. Look, Honey – about your present. I was going to get you a diamond wrist watch, with a gold band, and two rubies on the side.

ADELAIDE: Nathan, you shouldn't have.

NATHAN: It's all right – I didn't ... I'm sorry.

ADELAIDE *Gets in front of him – he puts his arms around her:* No, I kinda like it when you forget to give me presents. It makes me feel like we're married.

NATHAN: Don't worry, honey – one of these days I'm going to be in the money, and you'll have more mink than a mink.

ADELAIDE: Nathan darling. I can do without anything just so long as you don't start running the crap game again.

NATHAN *Fondly – backs away to R:* The crap game! What an absurd thought!
Benny and Nicely enter from R.

BENNY: Psst!
Nathan turns to him.
Twelve hundred cheesecake and fifteen hundred strudel.

NATHAN: Huh? *Moves to right.*

NICELY: Yesterday Mindy sold twelve hundred cheesecake and fifteen hundred strudel.

NATHAN: More strudel than cheesecake. That's great! That's my bet!

ADELAIDE: Nathan! What is this? *Moves to him.*

NATHAN: Nothing, honey, nothing. *Moves to her.*
Harry the Horse enters from L.

HARRY: Hey! Any news yet?

NATHAN *Speaks behind Adelaide:* Not yet, Harry, I'll let you know – later.

HARRY: O.K., Detroit. *Exit L.*

ADELAIDE: What was that about?

NATHAN: His wife's having a baby.

ADELAIDE: Why's he asking you?

NATHAN: He's nervous – it's his first wife. *Sees Sky Masterson in distance and moves round behind Adelaide pushing her to R.* Look, Adelaide, I'm expecting a fellow and I know you're hungry ...

ADELAIDE: Nathan, are you trying to get rid of me?

NATHAN *Push:* No, I just don't want your sandwich to get soggy. Fellows . . . Take her along to the drug store.

ADELAIDE *As she is being borne away by Benny and Nicely – they raise her up and exit R:* Nathan darling, you're so thoughtful. You're just the sweetest person. Good-bye.

Nathan is alone. He paces a moment, peers off. Sky Masterson enters L.

NATHAN: Hey, Masterson!

SKY: Nathan! You old promoter, you! How are you?

NATHAN: Fine, fine, Sky. You look great!

SKY: *Feel* great, Nathan. Two wonderful weeks out West in Nevada. Great place! Beautiful scenery, healthful climate, and I beat 'em for fifty G's at blackjack.

NATHAN: Fifty G's! . . . Going to be in town long?

SKY: No. Flying to Havana tomorrow.

NATHAN: Havana?

SKY: Yes, there's a lot of action down there. Why don't you come with me?

NATHAN: No, I got a lot of things to do . . . Meantime, how about dropping over to Mindy's for a piece of cheesecake? They sell a lot of cheesecake.

SKY: No thanks I'm not hungry . . . Tell me, how's Adelaide?

NATHAN: Oh, fine, fine. Still dancing at the Hot Box.

SKY: I suppose one of these days you'll be getting married?

NATHAN: Well, we all got to go sometime.

SKY: But, Nathan, we can fight it. Guys like us, Nathan – we got to remember that pleasant as a doll's company may be, she must always take second place to aces back to back.

NATHAN *His mind on other matters:* Yeah . . . Yeah. *Back to business.* Tell me – you hungry yet? Couldn't we drop over to Mindy's and have a piece of cheesecake or strudel or something?

SKY: No. I think I'll go get the late results. *Crosses to L. – takes scratch sheet from pocket.*

NATHAN: Oh! *Crosses to Sky.* But you will admit that Mindy has the greatest cheesecake in the country?

SKY: Yes, I'm quite partial to Mindy's cheesecake.

NATHAN: Who ain't? And yet there are some people who like Mindy's strudel.

Sky seems disinterested.

Offhand, which do you think he sells more of, the cheesecake or the strudel?

SKY: Well, I never give it much thought. But if everybody is like I am, I'd say Mindy sells much more cheesecake than strudel.

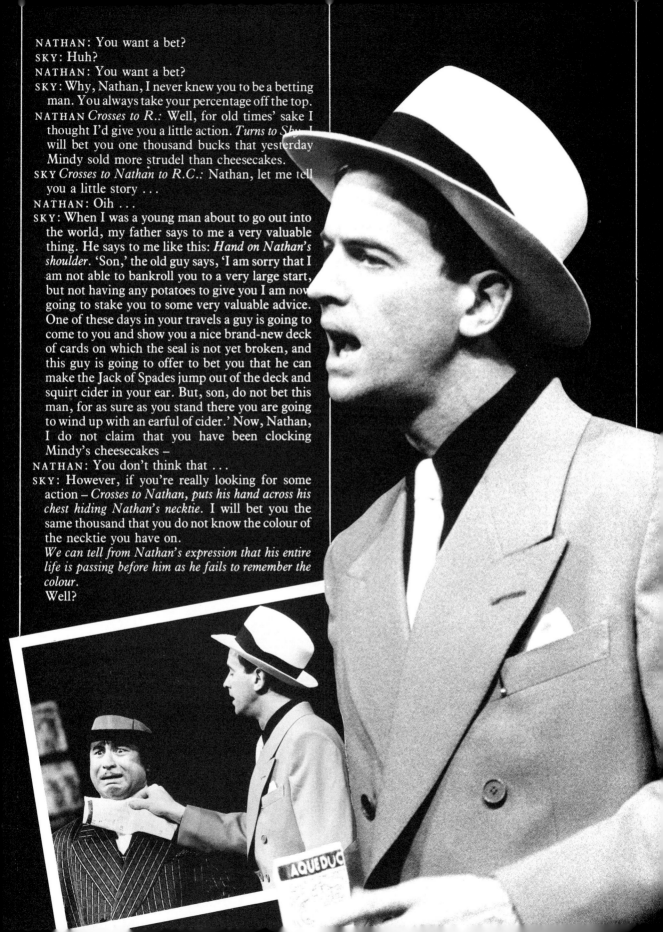

NATHAN: You want a bet?

SKY: Huh?

NATHAN: You want a bet?

SKY: Why, Nathan, I never knew you to be a betting man. You always take your percentage off the top.

NATHAN *Crosses to R.:* Well, for old times' sake I thought I'd give you a little action. *Turns to Sky:* I will bet you one thousand bucks that yesterday Mindy sold more strudel than cheesecakes.

SKY *Crosses to Nathan to R.C.:* Nathan, let me tell you a little story . . .

NATHAN: Oih . . .

SKY: When I was a young man about to go out into the world, my father says to me a very valuable thing. He says to me like this: *Hand on Nathan's shoulder.* 'Son,' the old guy says, 'I am sorry that I am not able to bankroll you to a very large start, but not having any potatoes to give you I am now going to stake you to some very valuable advice. One of these days in your travels a guy is going to come to you and show you a nice brand-new deck of cards on which the seal is not yet broken, and this guy is going to offer to bet you that he can make the Jack of Spades jump out of the deck and squirt cider in your ear. But, son, do not bet this man, for as sure as you stand there you are going to wind up with an earful of cider.' Now, Nathan, I do not claim that you have been clocking Mindy's cheesecakes –

NATHAN: You don't think that . . .

SKY: However, if you're really looking for some action – *Crosses to Nathan, puts his hand across his chest hiding Nathan's necktie.* I will bet you the same thousand that you do not know the colour of the necktie you have on.

We can tell from Nathan's expression that his entire life is passing before him as he fails to remember the colour.

Well?

NATHAN *Dismally:* No bet.

Sky removes his hand. Nathan looks disgustedly at the colour of his tie.

Blue. What a crazy colour.

Benny and Nicely enter.

BENNY: Nathan, we took Adelaide to the drugstore . . .

NATHAN: Don't bother me.

He pushes Benny who falls.

NICELY: Hi ya, Sky!

SKY: Good. How's it with you fellows?

BENNY: Not bad. *Rises.*

NICELY: Nicely, nicely. We took Adelaide to the drugstore, and she says for you to be sure to pick her up after the show at the Hot Box and *Don't be late.*

NATHAN: Yes, dear. I mean yes . . .

SKY: Yes, dear. That is husband talk if I ever heard it. Nathan you are trapped. In Adelaide you have the kind of girl that is most difficult to unload.

NATHAN: Maybe I don't want to unload her I love Adelaide. Besides a guy needs a doll. When a guy walks into a restaurant it looks nice if there is a doll behind him. A doll is a necessity.

SKY: Nathan, I am not putting the rap on dolls. I just say a guy should have them around when he wants them, and they are easy to find.

NATHAN: Not dolls like Adelaide.

SKY: Nathan, figuring weight for age, all dolls are the same.

NATHAN: Oh, yeah?

SKY: Yeah!

NATHAN: Then how come you ain't got a doll? *Crosses to Nicely.* How come you're going to Havana alone without one?

SKY: I like to travel light, but if I wish to take a doll to Havana there is a large assortment available.

Music: reprise of 'Follow the Fold'.

Mission Group is heard singing off stage L.

NATHAN: Not real high class dolls!

SKY *Turns to boys:* Any doll! You name her!

NATHAN: Any doll? And I name her! Will you bet on that? Will you bet a thousand dollars that if I name a doll you will take her to Havana tomorrow?

SKY: You got a bet! *Crosses to L.C.*

The Mission Group enters, singing, headed by Sarah. Two spectators follow them on. Sarah stops stage L.C. Nathan crosses to C. points to Sarah.

NATHAN: I name *her.*

SKY *Puts his hand to his ear, then withdraws it:* Her! Cider!

Interior, Save-a-Soul Mission

The Mission Band files in. Agatha, Calvin and Martha exit into Room R. Sarah goes down R. Arvide places bass drum up R. against window, hat on chair. Standing Stage C. is a painted sign in block letters. It reads: 'THERE IS NO PEACE UNTO THE WICKED' – PROVERBS 23, 9. Sarah puts tambourine on barber chair. Takes hat and coat off and places them on barber chair.

SARAH: Some day I'm going to take a pick-axe and rip up Broadway from end to end. *Sits at school desk and busies herself with papers.*
ARVIDE: Now, Sarah – angry words are not becoming to a missionary.
SARAH: You're right, Grandfather. I'm sorry. *Sits at desk.*
ARVIDE: Besides, they rip up Broadway every day. *Arvide crosses to armchair, picks up Mission newspaper which is in chair, sits and reads. Sky Masterson is seen on street through window. He has come from stage R. stops, and looks in through window when he has reached stage L. After a moment he enters through door to stage C. He assumes an air of repentance.*
SKY: Do you take sinners here?
ARVIDE *Rising and moving to Sky:* Indeed we do! . . . . . . Sarah!

SARAH *Rises:* How do you do?
ARVIDE: My name is Abernathy. Arvide Abernathy.
SKY: Sky Masterson. *And suddenly his head drops into his hands.*
SARAH *Crosses to Sky. Arvide moves towards Sky:* What's wrong?
ARVIDE: What is the trouble?
SKY: My heart is heavy with sin.
ARVIDE: You poor man.
SKY *Crosses, sits in armchair C. Sarah crosses D.L.:* I have wasted my life in gambling and evil betting. But now I suddenly realize the terrible things that betting can lead to. *A side glance at Sarah.*
ARVIDE *Calling:* Agatha! *Agatha sticks her head out of door R.:* Coffee!
Agatha exits, Arvide crosses D.L. of Sky.
SARAH: Didn't I see you a little while ago on Broadway?
SKY: Possibly. I have been wandering around, trying to get up the courage to come in here.
SARAH: And you're willing to give up gambling?
SKY: Gladly. I would never have become a gambler at all had I not fallen in with evil companions who were always offering me sucker bets.
Agatha enters with two cups of coffee on tray.
ARVIDE *Crosses down to Sarah's L.:* Here, young man.

SKY *Takes a sip of the coffee. Rises, crosses to Sarah:* Thank you. You know it makes me feel good just to talk to you people.

ARVIDE: You just go right on talking to Sister Sarah, and you'll be all right. I'm glad you found us.

SKY: The Bible says, 'Seek and ye shall find.'

ARVIDE: Very good. I wish we could find more sinners like you. We've been out every day trying.

SKY: Maybe you should try the night time.

ARVIDE: How's that?

SKY: Well, as a former sinner, I happen to know that the best time to find sinners is between midnight and dawn. You see in the daytime the sinners are all in bed, resting from their sinning the night before so as to be in good shape for more sinning later on.

ARVIDE: Oh!

SKY: Yes, you might even try having an all-night session against the Devil.

ARVIDE: A very good suggestion indeed! Thank you, Brother Masterson!

SKY: You're welcome.

ARVIDE *Drinks coffee:* Coffee is so good I can't understand why it isn't a sin. *Picks up paper and exits R. Sarah sits at desk. Sky places hat on single chair.*

SKY *Looking after Arvide:* Fine old gentleman. I suppose he sort of looks after you . . .?

SARAH: We look after each other.

SKY: Uh-huh. I suppose if either of you goes some place, the other goes along?

SARAH: Yes, of course.

SKY: Of course . . .

SARAH *Hands Sky pamphlet:* Here are two of our pamphlets I think you should read. They will give you a good deal of comfort.

SKY: Thank you.

SARAH: And we're holding a midnight prayer meeting on Thursday, which I'm sure you will wish to attend. *Rises, crosses to drawer at shoestand. Gets paper.*

SKY: I'm sure . . . Miss Sarah, I hope you will not think I am getting out of line, but I think it is wonderful to see a beautiful doll – I mean – a nice-looking lady like you, sacrificing herself for the sake of others. *Crosses two steps to R.* Staying here in this place, do you ever go any place else? Travel or something?

SARAH *Sits at desk:* I would like to go to Africa.

SKY: That's a little far. But there are a lot of wonderful places just a few hours from New York, by plane. Ever been in a plane?

SARAH: No.

SKY: Oh, it's wonderful . . .

SARAH: Here is another pamphlet that I think you should read. *Gives him pamphlet.*

SKY: Thank you ... Of course I will need a lot of personal help from you, you see. My heart is as black as two feet down a wolf's gullet.

SARAH: I'll be speaking at the Thursday prayer meeting.

SKY: I need private lessons. Why don't we have dinner or something?

SARAH: I think not, Mr. Masterson.

SKY: Sorry, just blossoming under the warmth of your kindness ... *Strolling around, looking the place over.* Hey ... *Crosses up C. to sign* ... That's wrong.

SARAH: What's wrong?

SKY: That's not Proverbs, it's Isaiah.

SARAH: It's Proverbs.

SKY: Sorry. 'No peace unto the wicked.' Isaiah, Chapter 57, Verse 21.
Sarah crosses to Bible stand, opens it. Behind his back Sarah looks up quotation in Bible. Slams the book shut.

SKY *Without turning:* Isaiah?

SARAH: Isaiah. *Sits at desk.*

SKY: There are two things been in every hotel room in the country. Sky Masterson, and the Gideon Bible. I must have read the Good Book ten or twelve times.

SARAH: You've read the Bible twelve times?

SKY: What's wrong with the Bible? Besides, in my business the strangest information frequently comes in handy. I once won five G's with a triple bet on Shadrach, Mischach, and Abednego.

SARAH: Tell me, Mr. Masterson, why are you here?

SKY: I told you. I'm a sinner.

SARAH: You're lying.

SKY: Well, lying's a sin ... Look, I'm a *big* sinner. If you get me, it's eight to five the others'll follow. You need sinners, don't you?

SARAH: We're managing.

SKY: Look, let's be honest. This Mission is laying an egg.
She is silent.
Why don't you let me help you? *Moves away.* I'll bet I can (*crosses R. a few steps*) fill this place with sinners.

SARAH: I don't bet.

SKY: I'll make you a proposition. *Picks up cardboard from chair, writes marker.* When did you say this big meeting of yours is – Thursday? I will guarantee to fill that meeting with one dozen genuine sinners. What's more I will also guarantee that they will sit still and listen to you.

SARAH: And what's my end of the bargain?

SKY: Have dinner with me.

SARAH: Why do you want to have dinner with *me*?

SKY: I'm hungry ... Here! (*gives her marker, she takes it*).

SARAH: What's this?

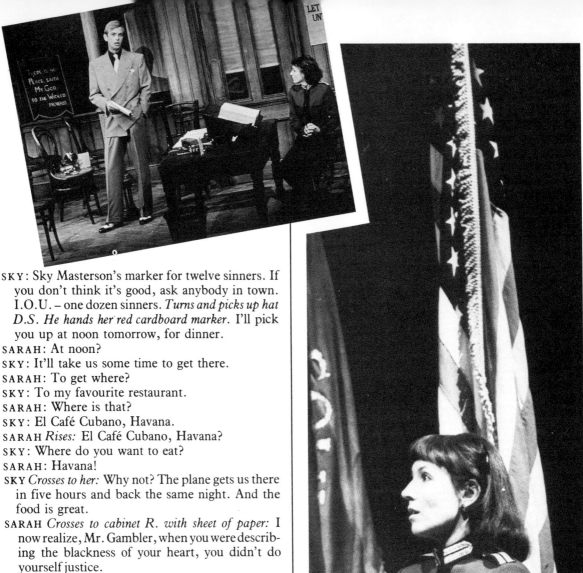

SKY: Sky Masterson's marker for twelve sinners. If you don't think it's good, ask anybody in town. I.O.U. – one dozen sinners. *Turns and picks up hat D.S. He hands her red cardboard marker.* I'll pick you up at noon tomorrow, for dinner.

SARAH: At noon?

SKY: It'll take us some time to get there.

SARAH: To get where?

SKY: To my favourite restaurant.

SARAH: Where is that?

SKY: El Café Cubano, Havana.

SARAH *Rises:* El Café Cubano, Havana?

SKY: Where do you want to eat?

SARAH: Havana!

SKY *Crosses to her:* Why not? The plane gets us there in five hours and back the same night. And the food is great.

SARAH *Crosses to cabinet R. with sheet of paper:* I now realize, Mr. Gambler, when you were describing the blackness of your heart, you didn't do yourself justice.
She opens drawer of cabinet, takes out typewritten sheet of paper. Sky goes to her and as he does he drops his hat on armchair.

SKY: And I now realize, Sister Sarah, that no matter how beautiful a Sergeant is, she's still a Sergeant.

SARAH: Please go away.

SKY: Why don't you change your pitch, Sarge ... 'Come to the Mission one and all, except Guys. I hate Guys!'

SARAH: I don't hate anybody.

SKY: Except me. *She looks at him.* Well, I am relieved to know that it's just me personally and not all guys in general. It is nice to know that somewhere in the world there's a guy who might appeal to the Sergeant. I wonder what that guy will be like.

SARAH *Slams drawer. Crosses to D.C.:* He will *not* be a gambler.

SKY *Crosses to her:* I am not interested in what he will not be ... I am interested in what he will be.

SARAH: Don't worry, I'll know ...

I'LL KNOW

SARAH *Sings:*
For I've imagined every bit of him
From his strong moral fibre
To the wisdom in his head
To the homey aroma of his pipe

SKY:
You have wished yourself a Scarsdale Gallahad
The breakfast-eating Brooks Brothers type!

SARAH *Spoken:*
Yes *Sings* and I shall meet him when the time
    is ripe.

SKY *Spoken:*
You've got it all figured out. Haven't you?

SARAH *Spoken:*
I have.

SKY *Spoken:*
Including what he smokes. All figured out,
    huh?

SARAH *Spoken:*
All figured out.

SARAH *Sings:*
I'll know when my love comes along
I won't take a chance
For oh, he'll be just what I need
Not some fly-by-night Broadway romance.

SKY *Crosses to her:*
And you'll know at a glance
By the two pair of pants.

SARAH *Crosses to R., passes him:*
I'll know by the calm steady voice
Those feet on the ground *He sits in single chair.*
I'll know, as I run to his arms
That at last I've come home safe and sound
And till then I shall wait
And till then I'll be strong
For I'll know when my love comes along.

SKY *Rises, crosses to her R.C. Shaking his head,*
    spoken: No, no . . . no . . . you're talking about
    love. You can't dope it like that. What are you
    picking, a guy or a horse?

SARAH *Spoken:* I wouldn't expect a gambler to
    understand.

SKY: Would you like to hear how a gambler feels
    about the big heart throb.

SARAH: No!

SKY: Well I'll tell you . . .

SKY *Sings:*
Mine will come as a surprise to me
Mine, I leave to chance – and chemistry.
Crosses two steps L.

SARAH *Speaks. Turns to him:* Chemistry?

SKY *Spoken – crosses back to her:* Yeah, chemistry.
Singing:
Suddenly I'll know, when my love comes
    along
I'll know, then and there
I'll know, at the sight of her face

How I care, how I care, how I care!
And I'll stop and I'll stare
And I'll know long before we can speak
I'll know in my heart
I'll know and I won't ever ask:
'Am I right? Am I wise? Am I smart?'
But I'll stop and I'll stare at that face in the
   throng
Yes, I'll know when my love comes along.

SARAH: I'll know.

SARAH AND SKY: When my love comes along.

SKY: *Kisses her*

They stand looking at each other as the music continues in the orchestra. Sarah is standing with her hands at her sides, she has been moved by Sky's lyric and is really fascinated by this cobra. Sky senses that he has made a dent in her defences. He puts his arms around her and kisses her tenderly. She submits to this but doesn't respond. He releases her and picks up his hat and crosses up L. by door. She stands, seemingly entranced. He stands watching her. She has been staring off into space. She turns to him. He looks at her in anticipation. She walks towards him, floating on air. He stands confidently anticipating another clinch. She reaches him and hauls off and belts him one across the chops . . . but really! Sky drops his hat. He reaches down and recovers it while rubbing his cheek.

SKY: I'll drop in again in case you want to take a crack at the other cheek.

He turns and exits L. Sarah moves down to desk.

Sarah looks at the marker, picks it up from desk and throws it into waste basket in front of desk and sings . . .

SARAH:

I won't take a chance
My love will be just what I need
Not some fly-by-night Broadway romance
And till then I shall wait
And till then I'll be strong
For I'll know when my love comes along.

3
A Phone Booth

The Arc spots come on and we find Nathan Detroit at the phone. During the following conversation Joey's voice will be heard over the speaker system from the theatre boxes R. and L.

NATHAN: Hello . . . hello, is this the Biltmore Garage?

JOEY'S VOICE: Yes.

NATHAN: Let me talk to Joey Biltmore.

JOEY'S VOICE: Who's this?

NATHAN: Nathan Detroit.

JOEY'S VOICE: This is Joey. What do you want?

NATHAN: Joey, I'm calling about the – er – *you* – know.

JOEY'S VOICE: The what?

NATHAN *Whispering:* The crap game.

JOEY'S VOICE: The. what?

NATHAN *A shade louder:* The crap game.

JOEY'S VOICE: Wait a minute, I got a customer.

NATHAN: Hurry it up, will you?

Three explosions over the phone, ending in one great big one.

JOEY'S VOICE: What did you say, Nathan?

NATHAN *Loud:* The crap game.

JOEY'S VOICE: Don't say that on the phone – suppose the cops are listening.

NATHAN *Whispering:* I'm sorry, the dice game . . . Look, Joey, is it okay if I use your place tomorrow night?

JOEY'S VOICE: If I get a thousand bucks.

NATHAN: I'll have it tomorrow.

JOEY'S VOICE: Then call me tomorrow.

NATHAN: Listen, Joey, if you're going to take that attitude I'll have the game some place else.

JOEY'S VOICE: So! Have it some place else.

NATHAN *Shouting:* Where else can I have it? . . . *Softening.* Joey, the dough is guaranteed. Would I lie to you?

JOEY'S VOICE: Yes!

NATHAN: I'm getting it from Sky Masterson.

JOEY'S VOICE: How do you know?

NATHAN: It's a bet – I can't lose. I bet him he could not take a doll to Havana.

JOEY'S VOICE: Why couldn't he?

NATHAN: Because she ain't the kind of doll that *goes* to Havana.

JOEY'S VOICE: Where does she go?

NATHAN: She don't go *no* place. That's why I know I'm gonna win.

JOEY'S VOICE: Don't be so sure . . . It ain't a horse, it's a doll . . .

NATHAN: But Joey –

JOEY'S VOICE: Nathan, there will be no crap game here tomorrow unless I get my dough in advance.

NATHAN: Joey, you've known me a long time.

JOEY'S VOICE: That's why I want it in advance.

NATHAN: Well, I can't talk no more – I got to meet Adelaide at the Hot Box. Look, just one thing. Can I tell the guys that the game is gonna be at your place?

JOEY'S VOICE: Not till I get my dough.

NATHAN: Okay, you'll get it. Goodbye!

JOEY'S VOICE: Goodbye!

NATHAN: I hope he gets stabbed by a Studebaker!

JOEY'S VOICE: You too!

4

The Hot Box, Nightclub

Discovered, Master of Ceremonies standing in front of microphone stage C. The place is well crowded.

MASTER OF CEREMONIES: And now for the Grand Finale of the Hot Box round-the-world revue, we take you down on the farm with our star Miss Adelaide and the Hot Box Farmerettes.

Dancing Girls enter from R. and L. in abbreviated Farmerette costumes with large hats and carrying rakes, hoes, pitchforks. There are two large pumpkins, two scarecrows on stage, after dance by girls Adelaide enters from R. carrying basketful of ears of corn she crosses to stage L. throws ear of corn to two spectators. Girl Dancer brings pumpkin down to stage L.C. Girl Dancer brings scarecrow down to R. of pumpkin. Girl Dancer gets two implements from two men stage L.

BUSHEL AND A PECK

ADELAIDE *Sits on pumpkin:*
I love you a bushel and a peck
A bushel and a peck and a hug around the
   neck
Hug around the neck and a barrel and a heap
Barrel and a heap and I'm talkin' in my sleep
   about you –
      GIRLS:
About you?
      ADELAIDE:
About you –
      GIRLS:
My heart is leapin', havin' trouble sleepin'
      ADELAIDE:
'Cause I love you a bushel and a peck
You bet your pretty neck I do –
Girls move heads from R. to L. eight times.
      ADELAIDE AND GIRLS:
Doodle, oodle, oodle, Doodle, oodle, oodle,
   Doodle, oodle, oodle, oo.
Girls change positions.
Nathan enters from stage R. sits on L. of table stage R. He calls to Adelaide. She crosses to him. Girl dancer looks for Adelaide, runs to her, taps her on the shoulder and Adelaide leaves Nathan to continue song, she yells 'Here chick, chick, chick,' throws her ear of corn to Nathan which he catches.
      ADELAIDE AND GIRLS:
I love you a bushel and a peck
A bushel and a peck, tho' it beats me all to
   heck
Adelaide slaps R. leg

ADELAIDE:
Beats me all to heck how I'll
Ever tend the farm, ever tend the farm,
When I want to keep my arm about you –

GIRLS:
about you?

ADELAIDE:
About you –

GIRLS:
The cows and chickens are going to the
    dickens –
All the spectators join in.

ADELAIDE
'Cause I love you a bushel and a peck
You bet your pretty neck I do—
Girls and Adelaide exit R.

ADELAIDE AND GIRLS
Doodle, oodle, oodle, Doodle, oodle, oodle,
    Doodle, oodle, oodle, oo.
Until they all exit

*Waiter enters from R. with cup of coffee which he
places on table front of Nathan, waiter crosses to stage
L. picks up pumpkin and takes it off stage L.*
*Waiter enters from stage L. with push broom and
starts sweeping up petals that were used in number by
dancing girls. Orchestra plays 'Home Sweet Home'
signifying the place is closing.*
*Patrons exit R. some a little tight, Nathan hums
'Bushel and a Peck' to himself as the Waiter is
sweeping up.*

NATHAN *Singing*
I love you a bushel and a peck, that lousy Joey
    Biltmore . . .
*Adelaide enters from stage R. dressed in dressing gown
carrying a cardboard box with 'Sally's Wedding Shop'
printed on it, also a book. She places cardboard box on
table R.*
*Nathan rises as Adelaide enters and throws ear of
corn upstage. He turns to Adelaide who rushes into his
arms.*

ADELAIDE: Hello, Nathan. *Placing cardboard box
    back of table. They embrace.*
NATHAN: Hello, pie-face.
ADELAIDE: How are you, handsome. *Slip back.*
NATHAN: Fine. What have you got there?
ADELAIDE: A book.
NATHAN: A book! You're always reading books.
    You're becoming a regular bookie.
ADELAIDE: Nathan darling, this is very interesting.
    The doctor gave it to me. I went to him about my
    cold. *Sits in chair with book in hand.*
NATHAN: Oh! How is your cold?
ADELAIDE: It's the same. *Sits.* So the doctor asked
    me how long I had had it, and I told him a long

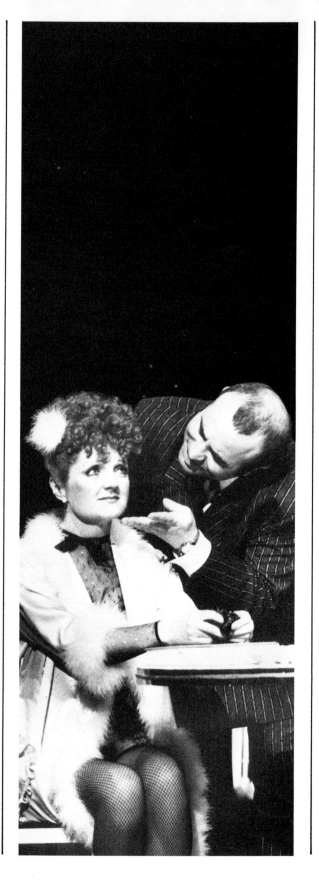

time, and I said I thought it was on account of my dancing with hardly any clothes on, which is what I usually wear, so he said to read this book, because he said it might be due to psychology.

NATHAN: You haven't got that, have you?

ADELAIDE: Nathan, this is the psychology that tells you why girls do certain kinds of things.

NATHAN: Would it tell you what kind of a doll would go for a certain kind of a guy which you wouldn't think she would do so?

ADELAIDE: What do you mean?

NATHAN: I'm just for instance! *Comes away two steps and turns to her.* There are certain dolls you

can almost bet they wouldn't go for certain guys.

ADELAIDE: Nathan, no matter how terrible a fellow seems, you can never be sure that some girl won't go for him. Take us.

NATHAN: Yeah.

ADELAIDE *Rises, places book on table, crosses to Nathan:* Nathan darling. Starting with next week, I'm going to get a raise. So with what I'll be making, I wondered what you would think, maybe we could finally get married.

NATHAN *Loosening his collar as he feels the strain:*

Well, of course we're going to, sooner or later.

ADELAIDE: I know, Nathan, *sneeze* but I'm starting to worry about my Mother.

NATHAN: Your mother? What about your mother?

ADELAIDE *Looks then speaks:* Well, Nathan, this is something I never told you before, but my mother, back in Rhode Island *sits in chair L. of table* she thinks we're married already.

NATHAN: Why would she think a thing like that?

ADELAIDE: I couldn't be engaged for fourteen years, could I? People don't do that in Rhode Island. They all get married.

NATHAN: Then why is it such a small state?

ADELAIDE *Look at him and hold:* Anyway, I wrote her I was married.

NATHAN *Standing:* You did, huh?

ADELAIDE *Each word coming through pain:* Uh, huh. Then, after about two years. *She comes to a halt.*

NATHAN: *What* after about two years?

ADELAIDE *In a very small voice:* We had a baby.

NATHAN *Crosses to L.:* You told your mother we had a baby? ADELAIDE *Rises, crosses to him:* I had to, Nathan. Mother wouldn't have understood if we hadn't.

NATHAN: What type baby was it?

ADELAIDE: It was a boy. I named it after *you*, Nathan.

NATHAN: Thank you.

ADELAIDE: You're welcome. *Crosses way to C.*

NATHAN: And – uh – where is Nathan, Jr., supposed to be *now*?

ADELAIDE: He's in boarding school.
He nods.
I wrote Mother he won the football game last Saturday.

NATHAN: I wish I had a bet on it.

ADELAIDE: But Nathan *turns away* that's not all, Nathan.

NATHAN *Crosses to her, a pause*: Don't tell me he has a little sister.

ADELAIDE: All those years, Nathan. Mother believes in big families.

NATHAN *Puts hands to ears*: Just give me the grand total.

ADELAIDE *Hardly able to get the word out:* Five.

NATHAN *Crosses to L.:* Your mother must be a glutton for punishment.

ADELAIDE *Crosses to him:* Anyway, Nathan, now we're finally getting married, and it won't be a lie any more.

NATHAN *A high moral tone:* Adelaide, how could you do such a thing! To a nice old broad like your mother?

ADELAIDE: But Nathan, you don't even know my mother?

NATHAN: But I'll be meeting her soon, and what'll I tell her? *Crosses to R. pass Adelaide* What'll I tell her I did with the five kids? Lost them in a poker game? What are we going to do?

ADELAIDE *Crosses to Nathan:* We could get married.

NATHAN: But marriage ain't something you jump into like it was a kettle of fish. *Feeling his collar again.* We ain't ready.

ADELAIDE: I'm ready, Nathan. *Crosses to table R. picks up box.* What do you think I got in this box? *Showing him box.* Nathan! What do you think I got in this box?

NATHAN *Reading cover of box*: 'Sally's Wedding Shop'. I can't guess.

ADELAIDE: It's a wedding veil. I've had it for three years. I won't show it to you, because it's bad luck . . . Would you like to see it?

NATHAN: It's bad luck.

ADELAIDE: So you see, Nathan darling, I got the veil. *Puts box down on table.* All we need now is our licence and our blood test.

NATHAN *Crosses to Adelaide.* Our what?

ADELAIDE: Blood test. It's a law.

NATHAN: What a city! First they close my crap game, then they open my veins.

ADELAIDE: Nathan, you're not planning to run your crap game again?

NATHAN: Adelaide, how can you think such a thing! Why do you think I give up the crap game. It's because I love you, and I want us two to be the happiest married couple that there is in the world. *Mimi enters half undressed, wearing a short robe.*

MIMI: Anybody see an earring out here? *She is searching the floor.*

ADELAIDE *Giving a perfunctory look:* I don't think so.

MIMI *Seeing Nathan:* You! I'm all dated up tomorrow with Society Max and he breaks it on account of your dopey crap game. Honest Adelaide, I pity you . . . *Sees earring on floor and picks it up.* Oh, here it is.
She exits R.

NATHAN: Adelaide, look at me. I'm down on my knees.

ADELAIDE *Turning away from him:* Oh, get up. It reminds me of your crap game. *Crosses to R. She sneezes.*

NATHAN *Crosses behind Adelaide to her R.:* Look, you're getting yourself all upset – after all everything is going to be all right. We love each other, and we're going to get married –

ADELAIDE: I don't believe you any more.

NATHAN: But it's true. You'll feel better tomorrow; come on, cheer up, honey. *He crosses to her and chucks her under the chin.* Let's see that old smile. *No response.* That's my happy girl. See you tomorrow.
She sneezes.
He rushes off R.
Adelaide crosses to table R. picks up book.

ADELAIDE *Reading:*

It says here

singing.

The average unmarried female, basically
    insecure
Due to some long frustration, may react
With psychosomatic symptoms, difficult to
    endure
Affecting the upper respiratory tract.

Looks up from book.

In other words, just from waiting around for
    that plain little band of gold
A person . . . can develop a cold.
You can spray her wherever you figure the
    streptococci lurk
You can give her a shot for whatever she's got
    but it just won't work.
If she's tired of getting the fish-eye from the
    hotel clerk
A person . . . can develop a cold.

reads again.

It says here:

sings.

The female remaining single, just in the legal
    sense
Shows a neurotic tendency, see note, *spoken*
note, note

Looks at note.

sings.

Chronic organic syndroms, toxic or hypertense
Involving the eye, the ear and the nose and the
    throat

Looks up, puts book down and rises, crosses down C.

In other words, just from worrying whether
    the Wedding is on or off.
A person . . . can develop a cough.

You can feed her all day with the Vitamin A
    and the bromo fizz
But the medicine never gets anywhere near
    where the trouble is
If she's getting a kind of name for herself and
    the name ain't 'his'
A person . . . can develop a cough.

And furthermore, just from stalling and
    stalling
And stalling the wedding trip
A person . . . can develop La grippe.

Back up to table.

When they get on the train for Niagara, and
    she can hear church bells chime

Sits in chair R. of table.

The compartment is air conditioned, and the
    mood sublime *Pounds box.*

Rises, crosses D.R.C.

Then they get off at Saratoga, for the
    fourteenth time
A person . . . can develop La grippe,
H'm.
La grippe,
La post nasal drip . . .
With the wheezes, and the sneezes.
And a sinus that's really a pip
From a lack of community property and a
    feeling she's getting too old
A person . . . can develop a bad, bad *cold.*

5

A Street Off Broadway

The Mission Band enters from L. and crosses from L. to R. They are playing 'Follow the Fold' Martha leads, carrying a sign, duplicate of the one we saw in 'Mission Interior', Scene 2, with the exception that it shows that 'Proverbs' has been rubbed off and 'Isaiah' substituted. Agatha is behind Martha playing the trombone, Calvin playing the cornet, Arvide the bass drum and cymbals, Sarah with her tambourine. Sky is patiently following along behind. Sarah, who is aware of his presence, gives an annoyed flounce as she gets to C. stage. Nicely sneaks on following Sky. He looks after them from stage L.C. as Benny follows on almost immediately. Nicely is still peering off stage R. as they all exit . . .

BENNY: Hey! Nicely! *Observing the direction of Nicely's gaze.* What are you looking at?
NICELY *Delighted, turning to Benny:* Sky was just following Miss Sarah, and you should have seen her. *He gives an imitation of Sarah's snootiness.* She give him a look that would have cooled off a moose at mating time.
BENNY *Crosses to R.:* Great! Just so he don't take her to Havana.
NICELY: Havana! He couldn't take this dame across the street . . . Where's Nathan? He ought to start lining up the game.
BENNY: I don't know, I suppose trying to see Adelaide. She's mad at him again. *Peers off, looks at wristwatch.*
NICELY: That Miss Adelaide. She is always taking his mind off honest work.
BENNY *Crosses to L. past Nicely.* Yes, it's too bad that a smart businessman like Nathan has to go and fall in love with his own fiancée.
NICELY: Benny, that is his weakness, and we should be tolerant, for I am told that is a world-wide weakness. Look. *Points out front.*

NICELY:

What's playing at the Roxy? *Takes Benny to stage C.*

I'll tell you what's playing at the Roxy

A picture about a Minnesota man, so in love with a Mississippi girl

That he sacrifices everything and moves all the way to Biloxi

That's what's playing at the Roxy.

BENNY *Hits Nicely in chest:*

What's in the Daily News?

I'll tell you what's in the Daily News

Shows paper to Nicely.

Story about a guy who bought his wife a small ruby,

With what otherwise would have been his union dues

That's what's in the Daily News.

Puts paper in pocket.

NICELY *Takes Benny to R. stage:*

What's happening all over?

I'll tell you what's happening all over.

Guys sitting home by a television set, who once

Used to be something of a rover

BOTH:

That's what's happening all over.

Love is the thing that has licked 'em

And it looks like Nathan's just another victim.

NICELY *Gesture with hand to sky.*

Yes sir, when you see a guy, reach for stars in the sky,

You can bet that he's doing it for some doll.

BENNY:

When you spot a John waiting out in the rain

Puts collar up.

Chances are he's insane as only a John can be for a Jane.

NICELY:

When you meet a gent paying all kinds of rent

For a flat that could flatten the Taj Mahal

BOTH:

Call it sad, call it funny,

But it's better than even money

Pound fists.

That the guy's only doing it for some doll.

BENNY *Leans on Nicely:*

When you see a Joe saving half of his dough

You can bet there'll be mink in it for some doll

NICELY:

When a bum buys wine like a bum can't afford

It's a cinch that the bum is under the thumb of some little broad

BENNY:

When you meet a mug, lately out of the jug,

And he's still lifting platinum fol-de-rol

Gesture with hand plucking.

BOTH:

Call it hell, call it heaven,

It's a probable twelve to seven

That the guy's *pound fists* only doing it for some doll.

A Guy and Doll enter R. She has a long cigarette holder. He carries a load of suit boxes and hat boxes. Stops L.C. He takes lighter from pocket and lights cigarette. She blows smoke in his face. She exits L. followed by Guy.

BENNY:

When you see a sport and his cash has run short

Make a bet that he's banking it with some doll.

NICELY *Crosses to L. of Benny:*

When a guy wears tails with the front gleaming white

Who the hell do you think he's tickling pink on Saturday night?

BENNY *Crosses to Nicely:*

When a lazy slob take a good steady job

And he smells from Vitalis and Barbasol

BOTH:

Call it dumb, call it clever,

Ah, but you can give odds Forever

That the guy's only doing it

For some doll,

Some doll, some doll,

The guy's only doing it for some doll!

Crosses to L. then stop, they both exit L. at finish of song.

Mission Exterior

It is around lunch time. The Mission Band enters from L. headed by Calvin who is carrying his cornet by his side. It is very obvious that he is tired and discouraged. Martha follows carrying the sign that we saw in the previous scene. She is not carrying it erect but at her side. Agatha is carrying her trombone listlessly, Arvide is carrying his drum by his side, also very discouraged and tired. Sarah follows on immediately behind Arvide and as she enters she is glancing offstage L. seeing if Sky Masterson is following her.

SARAH: Well, we finally lost him.

ARVIDE: I do think you should have paid some attention to him.

AGATHA: Yes, he attended every street meeting we had this morning. He must be interested in our work.

SARAH: Very.

AGATHA: By the way, you spoke beautifully this morning, Sarah.

SARAH *Disconsolately, crosses to Agatha:* No, I can't reach these people. I should never have volunteered for this post . . . Well, let's go to lunch. *Agatha, Calvin and Martha exit into Mission.* And I was going to convert Broadway all by myself. *Crosses towards Mission door.* I was going to take these gamblers and have them just begging to come to the Mission. *She sees Sky's Marker in trash basket, picks it up. She and Arvide are the only ones of the Mission Band who remain outdoors. General Cartwright, the head of the Save-A-Soul Mission enters from stage L. just as Sarah angrily throws Marker back into wire trash basket. She sees the General.*

SARAH: General Cartwright!

GENERAL: Good morning, Sarah. Arvide.

ARVIDE: Good morning, General.

SARAH: We didn't know you were coming to town, General.

GENERAL. I got in early this morning. I've spent the last hour trying to find you. *Agatha appears in the Mission doorway.*

SARAH: Oh, I'm sorry. We've been holding some extra street meetings, trying to stimulate more interest . . .

AGATHA: Good morning, General.

GENERAL: Good morning . . . Sarah, there's something I want to talk to you about.

SARAH: Won't you come inside, have some lunch with us?

GENERAL: No, I don't have time, dear. I have several other calls to make, Sarah, we at headquarters have come to a definite conclusion. We have decided to close this branch of the Mission.

SARAH: Oh, no.

ARVIDE: Close the Mission!

SARAH *Sarah crosses to L. pass General:* But, General, please! Someone can do good here, even if I can't.

GENERAL: Sarah, there are so many calls on us, so many other places where our work is really needed.

ARVIDE: But we are doing much better now.

AGATHA: We've announced a big meeting for tomorrow night.

GENERAL: You've announced a meeting! But will anyone be here? Will anybody come? *A second's pause, then Sky enters from R. with quiet dignity.*

SKY: Pardon me, I couldn't help overhearing . . . General, my name is Sky Masterson, former sinner.

GENERAL. How do you do?

SKY: How do you do? I wish to protest at the closing of this Mission. I believe Miss Sarah can be a big success here.

GENERAL: I am glad to hear you say that, but I'm not so certain.

SKY: A dollar will get you ten.

GENERAL: What! *Looks at Sarah.*

SKY: General, might I make a suggestion . . . *Goes to trash basket and picks up Marker which he conceals in his hat.*

GENERAL: Yes.

SKY: Why don't you come to the meeting tomorrow night and find out for yourself. *Crosses to Sarah and drops Marker in her tambourine, then crosses to R. Don't you think that would be a good idea?*

GENERAL: Well, if I thought the Mission had a chance . . .

SARAH *Looking at Marker in tambourine:* General, I personally guarantee you one dozen genuine sinners.

GENERAL: Hallelujah!

SKY: Hallelujah!

A Street Off Broadway

The crap shooters walk on . . . Harry the Horse is in the lead followed by Big Jule – after they are all on Benny enters from L.

BENNY *Crosses to R. then back to L.:* You all got your carnations?
Ad lib 'Yes'.
Remember, no one will be let in to the game without they got red carnations. It's like a pass word.
HARRY: Okay, but where's the game?
Exclamations from the mob, Nathan enters from R. Benny crosses to him.
Ad libs: 'Come on let's get going.'
BENNY: I'll tell you in a minute. Nathan, is it all set? Can I tell the guys that it's at the Biltmore Garage?
NATHAN: Not yet. I got to stall 'em for a while. Joey wants his dough first.
BENNY: But it's eleven o'clock, they won't stick around much longer.
NATHAN: So sue me. I left Nicely at my hotel to wait for the money from Sky. It'll be there.
Enter Nicely, eating sandwich, from R. Nathan crosses to him.
BENNY: There he is.
NATHAN: Where's the dough?

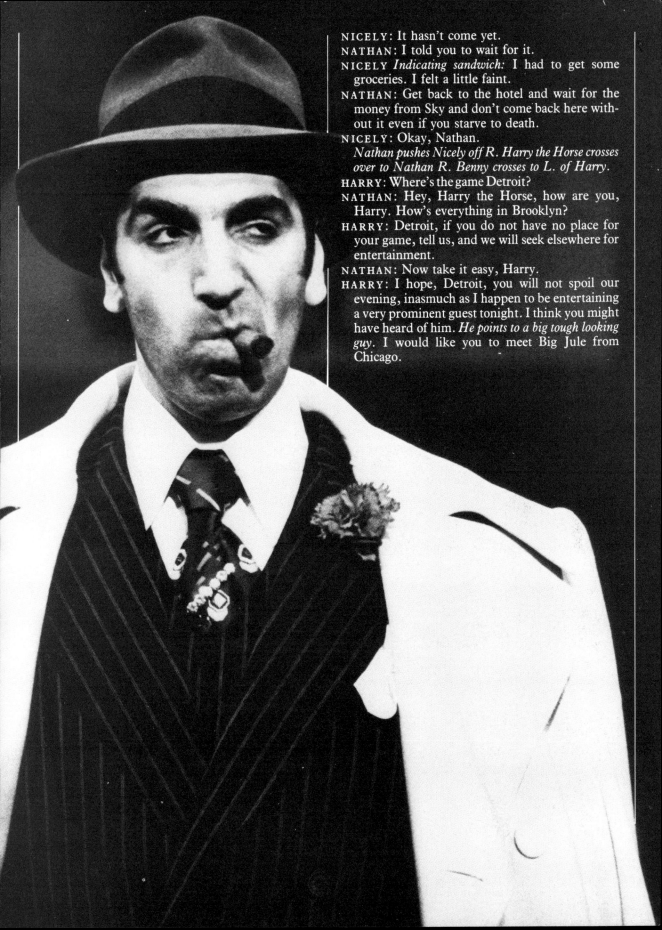

NICELY: It hasn't come yet.

NATHAN: I told you to wait for it.

NICELY *Indicating sandwich:* I had to get some groceries. I felt a little faint.

NATHAN: Get back to the hotel and wait for the money from Sky and don't come back here without it even if you starve to death.

NICELY: Okay, Nathan.

Nathan pushes Nicely off R. Harry the Horse crosses over to Nathan R. Benny crosses to L. of Harry.

HARRY: Where's the game Detroit?

NATHAN: Hey, Harry the Horse, how are you, Harry. How's everything in Brooklyn?

HARRY: Detroit, if you do not have no place for your game, tell us, and we will seek elsewhere for entertainment.

NATHAN: Now take it easy, Harry.

HARRY: I hope, Detroit, you will not spoil our evening, inasmuch as I happen to be entertaining a very prominent guest tonight. I think you might have heard of him. *He points to a big tough looking guy.* I would like you to meet Big Jule from Chicago.

Nathan crosses to Big Jule, Harry follows. Benny holds . . .

NATHAN *Very ingratiating:* Why, how do you do, Big Jule. *Shakes hands perfunctorily.* Welcome to our fair city, in which as you know the heat is on. But just be patient and you'll get some action. *Big Jule just stands there looking at Nathan.*

HARRY: What do you say, Big Jule, shall we stick around or shall we blow?

BIG JULE *Positively:* I came here to shoot crap. Let's shoot crap.

NATHAN: Sure, sure.

HARRY: Nathan –

Nathan crosses to Harry.

If there is no crap game tonight I am sure Big Jule will be considerably displeased; and Big Jule does not like to be displeased, as you can find out from those citizens who at one time or another displeased him. Although I will admit it is very hard to find such citizens in view of the fact that they are no longer around and about.

NATHAN: Why, Harry, you don't think I would be so rude as to displease a gentleman like Big Jule here, do you? *He puts his hand on Big Jule's arm.* Big Jule, believe me when I tell you that when Nathan Detroit . . . *He moves his hand and pats Big Jule on the chest. His words slow down as he feels Jule's gun. He removes his hand as though he touched a hot stove . . .* When Nathan Detroit arranges

something . . . you can count on it that . . .

He peters out as Brannigan enters from L. and crosses to the group. They are practically lined up for him and he looks them over very carefully.

BRANNIGAN: Well? Well? . . . an interesting gathering indeed. The cream of Society . . . Angie the Ox . . . Society Max . . . Rusty Charlie . . . Liver Lips Louie. *He walks up looking them over . . . goes down the line but nobody says anything.* Hey, Harry the Horse, all the way from Brooklyn, all . . . *Steps up, stops in front of Big Jule.* Pardon me, I'm very bad on names, but your face looks familiar. Mind telling me where you're from?

Big Jule chews his cigar a moment.

BIG JULE: East Cicero, Illinois.

BRANNIGAN: Oh, what do you do there?

BIG JULE: I'm a Scout Master.

BRANNIGAN: Well, don't ever help my mother across the street. *Smells flower in one of the mugs' lapel.* Mmm . . . lovely. *Looks over the line-up of flowered lapels.* This looks like a male chorus crosses, *D.L.* from 'Blossom Time'. What's the occasion? *His eyes travel over the entire group. They finally settle on Benny.*

NATHAN: Well, we . . . er . . .

BENNY: It's a party. We're having a Party.

BRANNIGAN: Indeed? What kind of a party? *At this moment Adelaide backs onto the stage from R. She is waving at some girls.*

ADELAIDE: Goodbye, girls, see you tomorrow. *Benny sees her and immediately gets his idea, he grabs Adelaide by the waist and leads her over to Brannigan.*

BENNY: It's a bachelor dinner. Nathan's getting married.

ADELAIDE: What!

HARRY *Grabbing Nathan and leading him forcibly to Adelaide and placing him with his arms around Adelaide. Nathan is obviously taken by surprise and shows off:* That is correct, Lieutenant! It's a bachelor dinner. Nathan's getting married.

BENNY: Yes, sir! *Sings.* For . . .

GROUP: . . . he's a jolly good fellow,
For he's a jolly good fellow
For he's a jolly good fellow . . .

BIG JULE *Steps down C.:* Which nobody cannot deny. *Slaps Nathan on back, almost upsetting him. Nathan lifts Adelaide to stage R.*

ADELAIDE: Nathan darling. I'm so thrilled! Why didn't you tell me?

NATHAN: It was a surprise.

ADELAIDE: But when I saw you standing here with all these fine gentlemen, I never dreamed it was a bachelor dinner. I thought it was a . . .

NATHAN *Suddenly jumping in:* Oh, it's a bachelor dinner.

BENNY *Also to the rescue:* It's a bachelor dinner.

NATHAN: Yes, sir! A bachelor dinner.

ADELAIDE: Just think after fourteen years I'm finally going to become Mrs. Nathan Detroit.

BRANNIGAN: Tell me, Nathan. When is the happy day?

ADELAIDE: When will it be, Nathan?

NATHAN: Well . . .

BRANNIGAN *Crosses to Benny:* Nathan, these good fellows are nice enough to give you a bachelor dinner. You should at least tell them the wedding date.

NATHAN *Shouts:* Well, we need time for a licence and our blood test.

EDWARD G ROBINSON
JOAN BENNETT
STARRING IN
"SCARLET STREET"
FULL SUPPORTING PROGRAM
DAILY MATINEES

ADELAIDE *Sighs:* Gee, wouldn't it be wonderful if we could be married tomorrow night. Right after the Hot Box.

NATHAN: Adelaide, we need time for a licence . . .

BRANNIGAN: You could elope.

NATHAN: What?

BRANNIGAN: You can drive upstate . . . what's the name of that place?

BENNY *Standing to R. of Brannigan:* Sing-Sing?

BRANNIGAN: No, no, Nathan, Buffalo. They'll marry you right away. They don't ask you for a blood test.

NATHAN: Ain't that unhealthy?

HARRY: Nathan, that's a great idea . . . elope. I'll lend you my getaway car. *He takes a quick look at Brannigan.* My Buick . . .

ADELAIDE *Throws her arms around his neck:* Oh, Nathan, let's do it.

NATHAN *Long pause . . . sighs:* Well . . . what the hell . . .

They embrace.

All congratulate them, ad lib.

BRANNIGAN: My congratulations too, Nathan. And I only hope there is nothing in heredity.

He exits L.

ADELAIDE: Nathan, darling, I got so many things to do before we elope. Will you be at the Hot Box tomorrow night?

NATHAN: I'll have a table reserved and I'll be all dressed up in whatever you elope in.

ADELAIDE: Oh, Nathan, I'm so happy. I ought to wire my mother Only what'll I wire her?

NATHAN: Send the telegram and date it back.

ADELAIDE: No, no, no. I'd better wait until we have five children. It won't take us long.

She exist R.

HARRY *Crosses R. to Nathan:* Nathan, you are indeed a lucky fellow. A most beautiful doll indeed. Do you agree, Big Jule?

BIG JULE: Tell me *to Nathan* how long you know the doll?

NATHAN: Fourteen years.

BIG JULE: Let's shoot crap.

BENNY *Darts over to Nathan:* Nathan, you'd better find a place!

NATHAN: How can I? The money from Sky ain't come yet.

BENNY: Maybe it won't come! Maybe Sky took the doll to Havana.

NATHAN: He couldn't have! How could he! She couldn't have gone!

Nathan anxiously counting them as they enter, Martha, carrying sign 'All Night Crusade Against The Devil', then Agatha, Calvin and Arvide. A pause, then Nathan places hand to head and collapses on Benny's shoulder.

8

Havana, Cuba – El Café Cubano

Music is blaring and dancing flaring. Sky ushers Sarah into the place R. but it is too much for her prim soul. She takes one look and flees. Sky must of course follow her. Stage lights fade to a blackout.

A fashionable couple dancing enter from R., they are picked up by the front arc spot. Immediately following them a unit on casters, with a table and two chairs is pushed in to marks at extreme stage R. This unit represents the Hotel Nacionale. Sarah and Sky are bowed into the place by the head waiter. As they enter they are picked up by the front arc spot. Sarah is seated R. of table and Sky L. of table. Sarah is handed an enormous menu by the head waiter. She looks the menu over.

SARAH: A ham sandwich!
  Waiter, Sky and Dancing Couple give her a quick incredulous look.
  Arc spot blacks out on Sarah and Sky. The platform unit is pulled off stage R. with Sarah and Sky on it to be reset with the Street Café.
  Dancing Couple dance off L. arc spot blacks out on them as they exit.
  Sarah enters with guide book in her hand followed by Sky. They are picked up by front arc spot as they enter and stop R.C. Sarah looks in guide book, then points towards audience supposedly to a monument tablet.
  First Tablet
SARAH: El Santo Cristo, the second oldest Mission in Cuba . . . Come on!
SKY: Where to?
SARAH: To see the oldest . . .
  Sarah walks to up centre stage, followed by Sky. She points towards audience as she looks in guide book.
  Second Tablet
  'Don't miss the Dungeons where prisoners were thrown to the sharks.'
SKY: Sounds like a million laughs.
  Sarah walks upstage then walks down stage L. as she looks her guide book over, Sky follows her obviously very tired. She points toward audience.
  Third Tablet.
SARAH: Here is buried Christopher Columbus.
SKY: At least he's lying down.
  Sarah starts to walk to stage R. when at this moment a very sexy Cuban Dancing Girl enters from R. followed by two Cuban Dancing Men. Sarah and Sky give them a quick glance as they pass by and exit L. A Waiter pushes on the unit which has been reset with a mantle and two chairs and a table. This represents a cheap street café. Sarah and Sky walk to stage R. She sits in chair R. of table, Sky in chair L. of table.
  A shoddy looking waiter stands at extreme R. waiting to take their order.

SKY: How about a drink?

SARAH: A milk shake please.

SKY *Holding up two fingers to waiter.* Dulce de Leche. *Waiter signals back with fingers knowingly. Sarah goes back to her guide book, to Sky's annoyance. Waiter returns with two drinks on cocoanut shells, as he serves Sarah he spills some on her dress which he quickly wipes off with a soiled serving napkin which he carries. Sarah sips drink as does Sky.*

SARAH *Sipping drink:* These are delicious. What did you call them?

SKY: Dulce de Leche.

SARAH: Dulce de Leche? What's in it – besides milk?

SKY: Oh, sugar, and a kind of native flavouring.

SARAH: What's the name of the flavouring?

SKY: Bacardi!

SARAH *Sips drink:* It's very good. I'll have another. *Arc lights black out.*
During the blackout Sarah and Sky pick up four empty cocoanut shells which were placed on platform. They place them on the table to denote they have had several drinks.

Sky is dancing his fingers on the table as the front arc spot picks them up. He tucks her under the chin. She brushes his hand away.

SARAH *Sipping her drink:* Doesn't Bacardi have alcohol in it?

SKY: Only enough to act as a preservative.

SARAH *A little tipsy:* You know; this would be a wonderful way to get children to drink milk.

Same Cuban Dancing Girl followed by the two Cuban Dancing Men that we saw before enter from stage L. They cross to stage R. doing their same sexy routine as they pass and exit R. Sarah rises and imitates their routine as she exits R. doing bumps. Sky rises and places hand to his head in amazement, quite shocked at her. Then he does the same movement as he exits R. Unit is pulled off stage R.

Cuban Girl and two Cuban Men enter from R. followed by Sarah pulling Sky on by hand. She is in a very gay mood.

SARAH *Shouting as she enters:* Two Dulce de Leche.
A waiter places a table extreme L. Sarah hands her cape to waiter who places it behind chair L. of table where Sarah sits. Sky sits at R. of table. Waiter brings two drinks in cocoanut shells which he places in front of them, also a wine bottle in a wine basket. This bottle is a breakaway bottle used by Sarah in fight at end of scene.

The solo female dancer begins to make up to Sky much to Sarah's annoyance. Sarah in retaliation dances with one of the Cuban men. Sky forces Sarah to sit down. Finally the Solo Dancer seizes Sky and makes him dance with her. Sarah takes Cuban by the hand and forces him to dance with her. Sarah becomes jealous, leaves Cuban and grabs Sky pulling him away from Dancer. Dancer strikes back, a free for all develops. A Cuban gets up on chair R. of table. L. and is about to throw stool at Sky. Sarah sees this, steps up on table, picks up wine bottle and breaks it over the head of the Cuban, breaking it to bits. Sky grabs Sarah over his shoulder rescuing her, and dashes out R. as the fight continues to become a brawl . . . Hanging blind breaks away . . . Stage lights fade out.

9

Outside El Cafe Cubano. Immediately Following

Sky enters from R. He is carrying Sarah in his arms and she is still struggling. He sets her down and it is apparent that she is a little tipsy.

SKY: Take it easy, slugger. It's over and you're still the champ. *She kisses him. She staggers after kiss.* Are you all right?

SARAH *Happily:* Am I all right! Ask me how do I feel . . .

SARAH *Sings: Arms around him.*
Ask me now that we're cosy and clinging
Well, sir, all I can say is,
If I were a bell I'd be ringing
Face front R. of Sky.
From the moment we kissed tonight
That's the way I've just got to behave
Boy, if I were a lamp I'd light
And if I were a banner I'd wave.
Places her head on his shoulder, crosses to L.
Ask me how do I feel,
Little me with my quiet upbringing
Well, sir, all I can say is,
If I were a gate I'd be swinging
He catches her as she leans to front.
And if I were a watch I'd start popping my
    spring
Or if I were a bell I'd go
Swings his arms over his head.
Ding, dong, ding, dong, ding.

Ask me how do I feel
Crosses to her L. puts head on his shoulder.
From this chemistry lesson I'm learning
SKY *Spoken:* Chemistry?
SARAH *Spoken.* Yeah, chemistry
                Sung
Well, sir, all I can say is,
If I were a bridge I'd be burning
Yes, *She backs him up to L.* I knew my morale would
    crack
crosses, backs him up to L. steps.
From the wonderful way that you looked
Boy, If I were a duck I'd quack
Or if I were a goose I'd be cooked
She falls on his chest.
Ask me how do I feel *He straightens her up.*
Ask me now that we're fondly caressing
Pal, if I were a salad
I know I'd be splashing my dressing
Puts hand down his face.
Ask me how to describe
This whole beautiful thing
Well, if I were a bell *Crosses to his L.*
I'd go Ding, dong, ding, dong, ding.
She falls into his arms at end of number.

SARAH: Havana is so wonderful. Why don't we stay here for a few days so we can see how wonderful it's really like.

SKY *Takes a moment*: I think we'd better hurry if we want to catch the plane back to New York.

SARAH: I don't *want* to go back to New York.

SKY: I'm *taking* you back!

SARAH: You're no gentleman.

SKY: Look, a doll like you shouldn't be mixed up with a guy like me. It's no good. I'm no good. *Sarah puts arms around him: he pushes her away.* You know why I took you to Havana? I made a bet? That's how you met me in the first place. I made a bet.

SARAH: Well, how else would a girl get to meet a gambler?

SKY *He picks up Sarah in his arms and carries her to stage L. She struggles.* Come on!

SARAH: No, no!

SKY: I got to think what's best for *you.*

SARAH: Oh, you talk just like a Missionary. *They exit L. as the lights black out.*

Sound of airplane is heard through the loud speakers and simultaneously a sign 'FASTEN SEAT BELTS' lights up a traveller. After a short interval the airplane fades out as does the sign.

10

Exterior of the Mission

It is four a.m. the following morning. Sarah enter L. she is minus her uniform coat and hat. She is in a very pensive mood. Sky follows on almost behind her also in a very thoughtful mood. He is hatless.

SARAH *Stopping stage C.:* Thank you for bringing me back. I must have behaved very badly.

SKY *At her side*: No, you were fine.

Adelaide enters from stage R. She is draped with assorted kitchen utensils given her at a shower. She is followed by four girls. They are carrying utensils given to Adelaide and humming 'The Wedding March'

ADELAIDE *Stopping with girls stage R.:* Oh, golly, I don't know how I'll get home with all this stuff. It was wonderful of you to give it to me.

She starts L., sees Sky, stops. Girls cross to stage L. then stop when Adelaide greets Sky.

Well, hello, Sky.

SKY: How are you, Miss Adelaide?

ADELAIDE: Oh, fine, Sky. Look! The girls just gave me a kitchen shower.

A drunk enters from stage L.

They went to an all-night drug store and surprised me with a kitchen shower! Look!

She waves utensils in the air. The drunk notices the brightness of the utensils.

DRUNK: I can't stand vulgar jewellery!

He exits R.

SKY: That's wonderful, Adelaide! ... You know Miss Sarah.

There are ad lib. greetings.

SARAH: How do you do.

ADELAIDE: Glad to meet you ... You know, Sky, we're eloping tomorrow night right after the Hot Box – Nathan and I.

SKY: Good luck.

ADELAIDE: Thank you, very much ... *Crosses to girls.* Gee, I feel just like a housewife, already. I'm going to love being in the kitchen, I've tried all the other rooms.

Adelaide exits stage L. followed by girls.

SKY *Looks off L.:* Miss Adelaide certainly seems happy.

SARAH: She's in love.

MY TIME OF DAY

SKY *Turns to Sarah:* Yeah. I guess so.

SARAH: What time is it?

SKY: I don't know. Four o'clock.

SARAH: This is your time of day, isn't it? I've never been up this late before.

SKY: How do you like it?

SARAH: It's so peaceful, and wonderful.

SKY: You're finding out something I've known for quite a while. *SKY Sings:*

    My time of day is the dark-time *At her L. side.*
    A couple of deals before dawn
    When the street belongs to the cop
    And the janitor with the mop
    And the grocery clerks are all gone
Moves D.C. stage with Sarah.
    When the smell of the rain-washed pavement
    Comes up clean and fresh and cold
    And the street lamp light fills the gutter with
      gold
    That's my time of day,
Sky front, Sarah turns to Sky.
    My time of day,
    And you're the only doll I've ever wanted to
      share it with me.
He crosses to R. pass her.

SKY: Obediah!

SARAH: Obediah! What's that?

SKY: Obediah Masterson. That's my real name. You're the first person I've ever told it to. *Turns to her.*

Sarah goes into Sky's arms and they embrace.

I'VE NEVER BEEN IN LOVE BEFORE
SKY *Hands on her waist:*
I've never been in love before
Now all at once it's you
Lets go of her.
It's you forever more
I've never been in love before
I thought my heart was safe
I thought I knew the score
But this is wine that's all too strange and
    strong
I'm full of foolish song
Takes her hands.
    And out my song must pour.
    So please forgive this helpless haze I'm in
    I've really never been in love before.

SARAH:
I've never been in love before
Now all at once it's you
It's you forever more
She crosses to L. face front.
    I've never been in love before
    I thought my heart was safe
    I thought I knew the score
    But this is wine that's all too strange and
      strong

I'm full of foolish song
And out my song must pour.
BOTH *He takes her hand and she turns to him:*
So please forgive this helpless haze I'm in
I've really never been in love before.
They kiss.
At end of number Arvide enters R. carrying his drum, he is followed by the Mission Band. They are obviously very tired from being out all night trying to convert sinners. Sarah sees Arvide as he enters, she goes to him as he is setting his drum down beside the Mission door.
SARAH: Grandfather! I thought you'd be asleep.
ARVIDE. Hello, Sarah dear. *To Sky.* Good morning, Brother Masterson.
SKY: Good morning.
ARVIDE: We followed your suggestion and stayed out all night *To Sarah.* We spoke to a lot of sinners ... Where have you been, Sarah?
SARAH: I've been to Cuba.
ARVIDE: You're even more tired than I am.
Offstage R. can be heard the clang of a police patrol wagon bell. A guy dashes on from R. at top speed. He runs across to the Mission entrance, sticks his head in the door and lets go with a loud piercing whistle, finger-in-mouth type, as the Missionaries and Sky react with surprise.

Music: The Raid.
SKY: What the hell is this?
Crosses to door. Benny, Nicely and Nathan come hurrying out of the door putting on their coats at the same time. They start off R. The lookout whistles at them and motions for them to go the other way. As they stop and turn, followed by Harry-the-Horse, the other crap shooters emerge, some with coats off, others just putting them on.

They start off and collide with Guys coming back, but they all exit L. As Nathan goes by, Sky grabs him but Nathan doesn't stop, he exits L.
SKY: Hey! What is this?
NATHAN: Canasta!
He dashes off followed by some of the Guys. Big Jule enters.
BIG JULE *Yelling to Nathan as he is running off L.:*
Wait a minute!
I'm losing ten G's.
He runs off L. The sound of the patrol bell has reached close up presence. As the bell stops clanging, Brannigan and two cops rush on from R. Brannigan stops short and realizes they have escaped him.
BRANNIGAN *To the two cops:* Someone must have tipped them off. Hurry up, Boys!
The two cops rush off L. Brannigan crosses to L.C. and stops, turns to Sarah.

Bell stops.
I seen a lot of strange things in my time but this is the first time I ever see a floating crap game full blast in a MISSION.
He runs on stage L.
SARAH *Stunned*: Crap game!
SKY: Sarah, you know I had nothing to do with this, don't you?
Sarah walks slowly toward the Mission entrance.
She stops.
SARAH *Turns away*: This wouldn't have happened if I hadn't – *She turns to him*. I never should have gone with you. It was wrong.
SKY: No, it wasn't. You went to help the Mission.
SARAH *Dully*: Did I?
SKY *Looks at her a moment*: Will I see you tomorrow?
SARAH: Everyone is welcome at the Mission.
SKY: That's not what I mean.
SARAH: It's no good, Sky. You said it yourself; it's no good.
SKY: Why not? What the hell kind of doll are you, anyway?
SARAH: I'm a Mission doll!
Music
Sarah goes into the Mission as the group follows her.
Slow curtain.

I

The Hot Box Nightclub

Stage lights dim up, the place is well crowded with patrons sipping cocktails. The M.C. is at stage C. standing in front of a microphone. This is all seen behind the translucent show curtain.

Music: 'Hot Box Fanfare'

M.C.: And now for the feature number of the evening. The Hot Box proudly presents Miss Adelaide and her Debutantes!

TAKE BACK YOUR MINK
Adelaide and Dolls

Music strikes up, show traveller opens as the balcony spots and front arc spot dim up. M.C. exits L. taking microphone with him. Four Dancing Girls enter from R. followed by Adelaide. Four Dancing Girls enter from L. They all carry long gold cigarette holders with cigarettes and are wearing golden gowns, shoes, hats, pearl necklaces and mink stoles.

ADELAIDE *Verse Stage C:*

He bought me the fur thing, five winters ago
And the gown the following fall, Then the
    necklace
the bag, the gloves, and the hat
That was – late forty-eight, I recall
Then last night in his apartment
He tried to remove them all (*crosses to R.*).
And I said as I ran down the hall:

1st Chorus. Crosses back to C.

Take back your mink
Take back your pearls
What made you think, that I was one of those
    girls
Take back the gown (*crosses to L.*), the shoes
    and the hat
I may be down, but I'm not flat (*crosses to C.*)
    as all that.

I thought that each expensive gift you'd
    arrange
Was a token of your esteem
Now when I think of what you want in
    exchange
It all seems a horrible dream –
So, take back your mink (*crosses 2 steps L.*).
To from whence it came (*crosses back to C.*).
And tell them to Hollanderize it
For some other dame.

ADELAIDE AND GIRLS *2nd Chorus:*

Take back your mink (*throw cigarette holders in
    orchestra pit. Take off mink*).
Take back your pearls (*take off pearls*).
What made you think that I was one of those
    girls – I'm screaming
Take back the gown (*take off Gowns*), take
    back the hat (*take off hats throw them
    upstage*).

I may be down, but I'm not flat as all that.
I thought that each expensive gift you'd
    arrange
Was a token of your esteem
But when I think of what you want in
    exchange
It all seems a horrible dream, (eek!)
Take back your mink
Those old worn out pelts
And go shorten the sleeves
For somebody else.

Adelaide and Dancing Girls go into their dance. At end of dance Adelaide and four Girls exit L. Four Girls exit L., then they immediately re-enter, running down-stage and gather up in their arms all the clothes that had been discarded during the dance.

ADELAIDE AND ALL GIRLS *Shouted. To the audience:*

Well! Wouldn't you?

Adelaide and four Girls exit L. Four Girls exit L.

After the number the lights come down and a single table is spotted. Sky enters from R. no hat, looks around like a man on the loose. He is unshaven again, and a bit crumpled. He drifts over to the empty table D.R. and sits down. A Waiter comes over from R. to Sky.

WAITER: Will you be with Mr. Detroit's party, sir?

SKY: Is he here?

WAITER: No, sir. Mr. Detroit has not been here all evening.

SKY: Bring me a rye and soda. *Sits L. of table. Waiter exit up R.*

Nicely enters from D.C. a bit furtively. Sits at table in R. chair.

NICELY *Picks up a stalk of celery and starts eating it:* Sky, did you see Miss Adelaide?

SKY: Huh?

NICELY: I bring for her a message from Nathan. I wish Nathan would bring his own messages.

SKY: What's the message? Where is Nathan?

NICELY: Well, it's this way. *He concentrates but still nibbles celery.* Nathan's aunt in Pittsburgh was suddenly taken ill with – er –

SKY *Wryly:* A rare tropical disease.

NICELY: Yeah, that's not bad.
Waiter enters from R. with highball on a tray, places it in front of Sky then exits L.
Anyway, Nathan has to –

SKY: Nicely, what is the message? Where *is* Nathan?

NICELY *Looks around to see if he's overheard then leans over towards Sky:* The crap game is still going on.

SKY *Casually:* Since last night.

NICELY: Big Jule being a large loser, does not wish the game to terminate. In fact, he is most insistent. So we find another place and the game goes on.

SKY: Where is the game?

NICELY: Are you looking for some action?

SKY: No, I'm leaving town tonight; but I do want to talk to some of the guys. You see, Nicely, I gave a marker to – well, somebody – and I'd kinda like to clean it up before . . .
He stops as Adelaide approaches from L. Adelaide crosses to Nicely. Nicely is on his feet quickly.

NICELY: . . . I'll meet you outside.

SKY: What about Nathan's message?

NICELY: Oh! *Getting it over quickly . . . Sky rises.* Miss Adelaide, Nathan is in Pittsburgh with a rare tropical aunt. Goodbye.
Rushes out R.

ADELAIDE *Crosses to R. looking after Nicely:* What? I don't understand. Sky, Nathan *has* to come here tonight. We're eloping to get married. Is it the crap game again?

SKY: You know Nathan. Why does it surprise you?

ADELAIDE *Sits R. of table:* But he promised to change.

SKY: Change!! Why is it the minute you dolls get a guy that you like, you take him right in for alterations?

ADELAIDE: What about you men? Why can't you marry people like other people do and live normal like people? Have a home, with – wallpaper, and book ends.

SKY *Sadly:* No, Miss Adelaide.

ADELAIDE: What do you mean, no?

SKY: Guys like Nathan Detroit, and – yeah, Sky Masterson – we don't belong in a life like that. So when dolls get mixed up with guys like us, it's no good. *He gets to his feet, places one dollar on table to pay for his drink.* No good – See you in a couple months. *Crosses to R.*

ADELAIDE: Where you going?

SKY: I don't know – Las Vegas, maybe. I got a ticket on the late plane.

ADELAIDE: Will you see Nathan before you go?

SKY: Maybe.

ADELAIDE: Tell him I never want to talk to him again and have him phone me here. *Sneezes and sniffles.*

SKY: Look! Why don't you find yourself another guy?

ADELAIDE: I can't. I love Nathan. Wait till you fall for somebody! You'll find out.

SKY *Looks at her a second:* Yeah.
Exits R.

ADELAIDE'S SECOND LAMENT
Adelaide Sneeze and then sings: Sitting:
In other words – just from sitting alone at a
  table
Reserved for two
A person can develop the flu
You can bundle her up in her woollies,
And I mean the warmest brand,
You can wrap her in sweaters and coats
'Til it's more than her frame can stand
If she still gets the feeling she's naked
From looking at her left hand –
A person can develop the flu
Huh! The flu! A hundred and three point two
So much virus inside
That her microscope slide
Looks like a day at the zoo!
Just from wanting her memories in writing
And a story her folks can be told
A person can develop a cold.
She sneezes.
Blackout

2

Forty Eighth Street

Manhole rail is at stage R.C. Edison blinker wagon with light blinking at stage L.C. A box is at L. of wagon. Sarah sits on this box when Arvide sings to her. Sarah enters from R. at a brisk pace, Arvide is following her, carrying his bass drum and having quite a time keeping up with Sarah.

ARVIDE: Not so fast, Sarah, not so fast.
> *Puts drum down, Sarah stops stage C.*

Look, suppose we don't have a big meeting tonight, suppose nobody is there at all. We'll explain to the General.

SARAH: We won't have to explain, it'll be very clear. *Crosses to L.* I just want to get away from this whole place. To go someplace where – where –

ARVIDE: Where the sinners are all respectable and well behaved?

SARAH: You saw what happened last night. They gambled in our Mission.

ARVIDE: And some day they'll be praying there. Even a man like Sky Masterson. He came seeking refuge.

SARAH: He came seeking *me.* Did you know that?

ARVIDE: Are you kidding? I knew that the minute he started picking on you. *He picks up his bass drum and goes toward Sarah.* But I didn't know you were going to get stuck on him.

SARAH *Crosses to front of blinker wagon:* I'll get over it.

ARVIDE *Crosses to L. passes Sarah:* What do you want to get over it for? It isn't pneumonia.

SARAH: The man I love will not be a gambler.

ARVIDE *Putting down drum up L.:* But if you love him enough –

SARAH: He will not be a gambler.

ARVIDE: Sarah, dear.

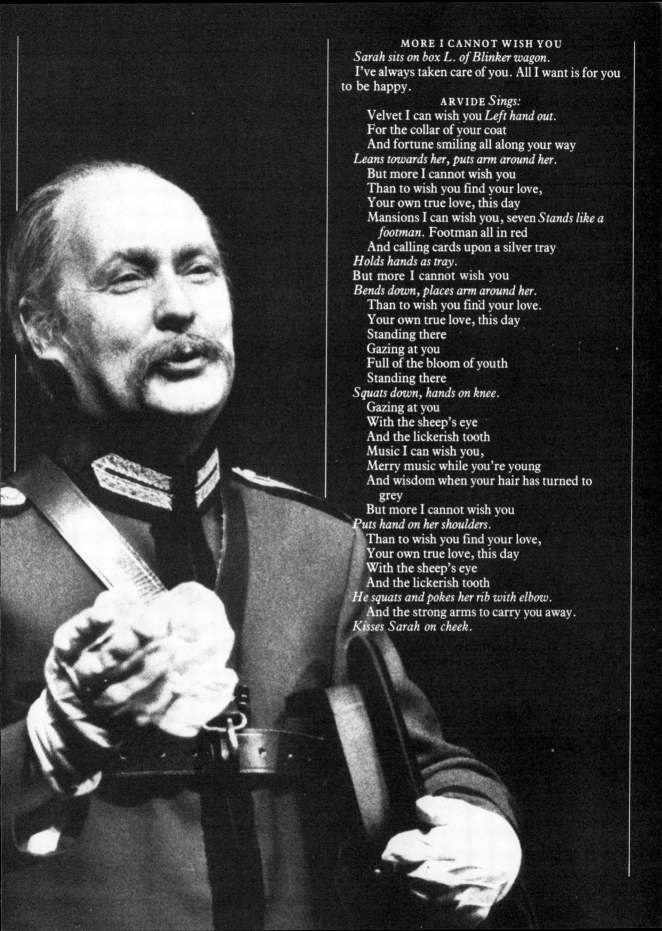

MORE I CANNOT WISH YOU

Sarah sits on box L. of Blinker wagon.

I've always taken care of you. All I want is for you
to be happy.

ARVIDE *Sings:*

Velvet I can wish you *Left hand out.*
For the collar of your coat
And fortune smiling all along your way
Leans towards her, puts arm around her.
But more I cannot wish you
Than to wish you find your love,
Your own true love, this day
Mansions I can wish you, seven *Stands like a*
footman. Footman all in red
And calling cards upon a silver tray
Holds hands as tray.
But more I cannot wish you
Bends down, places arm around her.
Than to wish you find your love.
Your own true love, this day
Standing there
Gazing at you
Full of the bloom of youth
Standing there
Squats down, hands on knee.
Gazing at you
With the sheep's eye
And the lickerish tooth
Music I can wish you,
Merry music while you're young
And wisdom when your hair has turned to
  grey
But more I cannot wish you
Puts hand on her shoulders.
Than to wish you find your love,
Your own true love, this day
With the sheep's eye
And the lickerish tooth
He squats and pokes her rib with elbow.
And the strong arms to carry you away.
Kisses Sarah on cheek.

Sky enters with Nicely L. Nicely crosses to manhole rail, leans on it. Sky stops L. Sarah rises.

SKY: Good evening, Miss Sarah. Well, Brother Abernathy, how goes it with the Soul-saving? Tonight's the big meeting, isn't it?

ARVIDE: It's supposed to be. The General is coming, and she's expecting – uh . . .

SKY: Well, very few people will be there, in fact, nobody. And uh . . .

SARAH *Crosses to L., passes Sky:* I don't think Mr. Masterson is interested in our troubles, Grandfather. We've got to hurry.

Arvide picks up drum.

SKY: Miss Sarah.

She stops.

You've forgotten something, but being a gambler, I never forget things like this. You hold my marker for twelve sinners tonight.

SARAH: Thank you, Mr. Masterson, but I'd rather you forgot about it.

SKY: I cannot welch a marker.

SKY: Mr. Masterson, last night the Mission was filled with your friends. Let us say we're even.

She exits L.

Arvide, passing Sky on the way out, whispers out of the corner of his mouth.

ARVIDE: If you don't pay off on that marker I'll tell the whole town you're a dirty welcher.

He exits L.

SKY *Crosses to Nicely:* Nicely! Where's the crap game?

NICELY: It's about ten minutes' walk from here.

SKY: Which way?

NICELY: This way! *He starts down the manhole.*

Blackout.

3

Crap Game in the Sewer

The stage lights dim up behind No. 1 trans. show traveller revealing the Crap Game Dance. No. 1 traveller opens, Balcony spots dim on.

There is a crap shooter sitting on pipe up R. Harry the Horse and a crap shooter are standing on the platform R.C. upstage.

Two crap shooters are hanging on ladder upstage C. watching the dance.

Benny, Angie the Ox, Big Jule, Society Max and one other crap shooter are standing on platform up L.C.

Nathan Detroit is standing in front of platform L.C. Crosses L.C.

When the dance is finished all the crap shooters move downstage, putting their coats on and some are putting ties on. They all wear red carnations. Most of them are getting ready to leave the game.

BIG JULE: Wait a minute. Where you all going. I
    came here to shoot crap.
PLAYER: We had enough.
    Ad libs. from the crowd.
ANOTHER PLAYER: Let's go home.

NATHAN: You see, Big Jule, the boys are slightly fatigued from weariness, having been shooting crap for quite a long while now, namely twenty-four hours.

Ad libs. from crowd.

BIG JULE: I do not care who is tired. I am out twenty-five G's so nobody leaves. *He moves to Nathan and pats his shoulder revolver threateningly.*

NATHAN: Gentlemen, I begin to see the logic of Big Jule. It is not that Big Jule is a bad loser; it is merely that he prefers to win. Right, Big Jule?

BIG JULE: Give me the dice. I'm shooting five hundred.

BENNY: I'll take two hundred.

The players are a little slow in getting their money up and they all groan.

PLAYER: I'm half dead.

HARRY: If you do not shut up, Big Jule will arrange the other half.

Players put their money up quickly.

BIG JULE *As he rolls:* Hah!

NATHAN: And it's a one and a one. Snakes eyes. You lose. *Ad lib. Reaches for his take.* And fifty dollars for the house. *Crosses to table.* But the dice are still yours, and your luck is bound to . . .

BIG JULE: Shut up!

NATHAN: . . . to change.

BIG JULE: Five hundred more.

BENNY: Two hundred more.

The Guys cover him again, but very reluctantly.

NATHAN: And here comes that big lucky roll.

BIG JULE *As he throws:* Haaah!

NATHAN: And it's – snake eyes again.

They all grab their money.

BENNY: Tough luck, Big Jule.

BIG JULE: Well, that cleans me.

Ad lib. and general relaxing, even expressions of pleasure.

But I ain't through yet.

General apprehension. Ad lib.

I will now play on credit.

Many moans, ad lib.

NATHAN: You see, Big Jule, the boys are all pretty tired. Of course me, personally, I am fresh as a daisy.

BIG JULE: Then I will play with *you*.

NATHAN: Me?

BIG JULE: Yeah, you. You been rakin' down out of every pot, you must have by now quite a bundle.

NATHAN: Well, being I assume the risk it is only fair I should assume some of the dough.

BIG JULE: Detroit, I am going to roll you, Willy or Nillie. If I lose, I will give you my marker. *Starts writing.*

NATHAN: And if I lose?

HARRY: You will give him cash.

NATHAN: Let me hear it from Big Jule.

BIG JULE: You will give me cash.

NATHAN: Now I heard it.

Benny crosses down L., back of Nathan.

BIG JULE: Here is my marker.

Nathan looks at it, then at Big Jule.

Put up your dough. Is anything wrong?

NATHAN: No, no. 'I.O.U. one thousand dollars.' Signed X! *Reaching into his pocket.* How is it you can write one thousand, but you cannot write your signature?

BIG JULE: I was good in Arithmetic, but I stunk in English.

NATHAN: *His money now out, puts it down:* Here! This will put you through Harvard.

BIG JULE: I'm rolling a thousand. And to change my luck I will use my own dice.

NATHAN *Horrified:* Your own dice!

BIG JULE: I had them made especially for me in Chicago.

NATHAN: Big Jule, you cannot interpolate Chicago dice in a New York crap game.

BENNY: That is a breach of etiquette.

HARRY: Show me where it says that in Hoyle.

NATHAN: Not that I wish to seem petty, but could I see these dice?

All men crowd around looking at dice. Big Jule takes them out, gives them to Nathan.

NATHAN: But these – these dice ain't got no spots on 'em. They're blank.

BIG JULE: I had the spots removed for luck. But I remember where the spots formerly were.

NATHAN: You are going to roll blank dice and call 'em from remembering where the spots formerly was?

BIG JULE *Threateningly:* Why not? *Pulls Nathan up by coat.*

NATHAN *Wipes perspiration from his forehead:* I see no reason.

BIG JULE *He rolls:* A five, and a five. My point is ten.

NATHAN: Well, I still got a chance.

BIG JULE *Shaking the dice:* Tensy! Tensy! Come againsy!

NATHAN: I wish he'd fall down on his endsy.

BIG JULE: Heah! *He rolls.* A ten! I win!

NATHAN: A ten?

BIG JULE *Pointing:* A six and a four.

NATHAN *Looking:* Which is the six and which is the four?

BIG JULE: Either way . . . *Picks up dice.* Now I'm shooting two thousand. Get it up!

NATHAN *Looks at his watch:* I just remembered. I'm eloping tonight. Adelaide is waiting for me. *Starts to exit. Big Jule grabs him and pulls him back.*

BIG JULE: Get up two thousand.

NATHAN: How about letting the other guys in on the fun?

Ad lib. 'Ah no.'

BIG JULE: After I'm through with you! ... Two thousand.

Nathan puts it up, reluctantly. Big Jule shakes dice, rolls.

Haah! Seven! I win.

NATHAN *Swallowing hard:* What a surprise.

BIG JULE *Picks up dice:* Detroit, I think I will take it easy this time.

NATHAN: What do you mean?

BIG JULE: I am shooting one dollar.

NATHAN: I'll take all of it.

Big Jule puts it down.

BIG JULE *Rolls:* How do you like that? Snake eyes! I lose.

NATHAN: For this I got to bend down.

BIG JULE: Detroit, now I will give you a chance. I will roll for you three thousand.

NATHAN: Three G's.

BIG JULE *Picks up dice, firm:* I am rolling you for three G's. Put it down there.

Nathan counts out the money. Puts his hands over his eyes as Big Jule starts to roll.

NATHAN: Wouldn't it be more convenient if I put it right into your pocket?

BIG JULE: Get it up? *Rolling.* Haaah! Eleven. I win.

NATHAN: That cleans me.

BIG JULE *To the others, picks up dice and money:* Now I will play with *you* guys.

Ad lib.

NATHAN: Wait a minute! You gotta give me a chance to get even. I will roll *you*, with my dice.

BIG JULE: All right, Detroit, that's fair. What are you gonna use for money?

NATHAN: I will give you my marker.

HARRY: And you want Big Jule to put up cash?

BENNY: Nathan did it.

NATHAN: Sure I done it. What kind of a deal is this, anyway?

BENNY: Take it easy, Nathan.

NATHAN: Him with his no-spot dice! Somebody ought to knock the spots off *him. Stands right up to Big Jule.*

HARRY: Nathan, don't make Big Jule have to do something to you.

BIG JULE: Yeah, I am on my vacation.

NATHAN: Go ahead, shoot me. Put me in cement. At least I would know where I am. Here I risk my neck to set up a crap game. I even promise to get married on account of it. So look how I wind up. Broke in a sewer. Believe me, my tough friend from Chicago, there is nothing you could do to me that would not cheer me up.

Nicely comes down the stairs.

NICELY *Motioning to someone:* Here they are.

Sky comes down.

SKY: Good evening, gentlemen.

BIG JULE *Crosses to Sky:* Well, fresh blood. You looking for some action?

SKY: Not at the moment. I would like to talk to some of you guys.

BIG JULE: We ain't talking. We're shooting crap.

SKY *Quietly:* I am asking for only one minute.

BIG JULE: I said we are shooting crap.

SKY: It has to do with Miss Sarah Brown's Mission.

BIG JULE: Say, who is this guy?

HARRY: It's the fellow I was telling you, took the Mission doll to Havana.

BIG JULE: Oh, I get it. Look, fellow, why don't you go back to your praying tomato? You're slowing up the action around here.

SKY *Smoothly:* If you want some action, would you like to make a small wager on a proposition?

BIG JULE: What's the proposition?

SKY: Am I right-handed or left-handed?

BIG JULE: How would I know a thing like that?

SKY: I'll give you a clue.

Socks Big Jule with a right [ad libs.]. Big Jule goes down. Staggers to his feet, reaching groggily for his gun. Sky gets it first, tosses it to Nathan who catches it gingerly.

HARRY: Heh! *Rises, crosses upstage.*

NATHAN *Handing gun to Benny:* Here, put this back in the ice box.

SKY *Addressing the group:* Look, you guys. *Crosses to Nathan.* Tonight in Miss Sarah Brown's Mission at 409 West 49th Street they are holding a midnight prayer meeting. I promised I would deliver to them some sinners, and when it comes to sinning most of you guys are high up among the paint cards.

Everyone looks very uncomfortable, ad lib.

HARRY: I don't want to waste no evening in a Hallelujah joint.

SKY: If you won't do it as a favour to me, do it as a favour to yourselves. I guarantee you the air in the Mission smells cleaner than down here . . .

Ad libs.

. . . and maybe it would not hurt you guys to learn something else besides the odds on making a four the hard way.

HARRY: You been reading the Bible too much.

SKY: So what? Maybe the Bible don't read as lively as the Scratch Sheet, but it is at least twice as accurate.

They only mumble with heads hung low, ad lib.

Well, I tried . . . See you around, Nathan.

NATHAN *Turns to Sky:* Oh, oh, Sky . . . About that Havana business, I regret I temporarily do not have the one thousand to pay you.

SKY: You don't have to pay me. *Pulls out a bill.* You won.

NATHAN: But I thought you took Miss Sarah to Havana.

SKY: You thought wrong. *Giving money to Nathan he starts up the ladder.*

NATHAN: Come on, Big Jule, get up. I have now got dough to roll you again. But with my dice.

HARRY *On his feet again:* Nothing doing. With those dice he cannot make a pass to save his soul.

SKY *Stops dead on ladder:* What'd you say?

HARRY *Belligerently:* I says with them dice he cannot make a pass to save his soul.

SKY *Crosses to Nathan's R., slowly as he returns to them:* Well, maybe I can make a pass to save yours ... *Pointing to one, then another.* ... And yours ... and his ...
From the group: 'Huh? ... What are you talking about?' Ad lib.
I am going to roll the dice. I will bet each of you a thousand dollars against your souls. One thousand cash against a marker for your souls.
Big Jule rises, ad lib.
If I win, you guys all show up at the Mission tonight.
There is a buzz of interest, ad lib.
Is it okay?
Ad lib.

HARRY: Let me get this. If you lose, we each get a thousand bucks, and if you win we gotta show up at the Mission doll's cabaret?

SKY *Tight-lipped:* If I win you guys show up at the Save-A-Soul Mission. One meeting.

HARRY *Thinks a minute:* Okay by me.

BENNY *Taking the lead:* By me too.
The others agree, as they all start writing markers.

100

Benny also writes.

SKY *As the others hand him their markers:* You too, Nathan. A thousand dollars against your soul.

NATHAN: Me? I don't even know if I got one.

SKY: You got one some place.

NATHAN: How do you spell 'soul'?

BENNY *Spelling:* S – o –
Nathan pushes Benny.
Sky backs upstage.

SKY: All right, put down your markers.
They do so. Sky covers them all with a one thousand dollar bill.
Give me the dice.
Some men squat down.
He gets them.
And give me room. *He hesitates, nervously.*
Tosses the dice in his hand once or twice.

A PLAYER: Come on, quit stallin', roll.
Men squatting rise.

HARRY: What's the matter, Sky, turning chicken?

SKY: You've seen me roll for a hundred G's. But I've got a little more than dough riding on this one.
Walks D.C.

SKY O.C.:
They call you Lady Luck
But there is room for doubt
At times you have a very un-ladylike way of
    running out
Takes 2 steps D.C.
    You're on this date with me
    The pickings have been lush
    And yet before this evening is over
    You might give me the brush
Crosses 3 steps R.
    You might forget your manners
    You might refuse to stay, and so
    The best that I can do is pray.
1st Chorus.
At R.C.
    Luck be a lady tonight
    Luck be a lady tonight.
    Luck, if you've ever been a lady to begin with
    Luck, be a lady tonight.
Crosses 2 steps L.
    Luck, let a gentleman see
    How nice a dame you can be
    I know the way you've treated other guys
        you've been with,
    Luck be a lady with me.

Crosses 2 steps L.
A lady doesn't leave her escort
It isn't fair, it isn't nice.
A lady doesn't wander all over the room
And blow on some other guy's dice.
So let's keep the party polite
Take roll of money out of pocket.
Never get out of my sight
Stick with me, baby, I'm the fellow you came
   in with
Luck be a lady *Throws money on floor.*
Luck be a lady *Throws more money on floor.*
Luck be a lady tonight.
Crosses to R.

Sky goes to stage R., motions to Big Jule to put up his marker then motions to crap shooter upstage R. Big Jule and crap shooter move to C. Sky crosses to C., motions to crap shooter who moves down C. Then Sky motions to crap shooter L.C. Crap shooter moves down C. Sky comes to stage C.

2nd Chorus.
> ENSEMBLE:
Luck be a lady tonight
Luck be a lady tonight.
Luck, if you've ever been a lady to begin with
Luck be a lady tonight.
> SKY:
Luck, let a gentleman see *Men kneel.*
> ENSEMBLE:
Luck, let a gentleman see
> SKY:
How nice a dame you can be
> ENSEMBLE:
How nice a dame you can be
> SKY:
I know the way you've treated other guys
   you've been with.
> ENSEMBLE:
Luck be a lady, a lady, be a lady with me.
Crap shooter crosses down L.C.

> SKY:
Luck be a lady with me
A lady wouldn't flirt with strangers
She'd have a heart, she'd have a soul.
A lady wouldn't make little snake-eyes at me
> ENSEMBLE:
Roll 'em, roll 'em, roll 'em, snake-eyes
> SKY:
When I've bet my life on this roll.
All men squat.
> ENSEMBLE:
Roll 'em, roll 'em, roll 'em.
> SKY:
So let's keep the party polite

> ENSEMBLE:
So let's keep the party polite
> SKY:
Never get out of my sight
> ENSEMBLE:
Never get out of my sight
Stick here, baby, stick here, baby.
> SKY:
Stick with me, baby, I'm the fellow you came
   in with,
Luck be a lady
> ENSEMBLE:
Luck be a lady
> SKY:
Luck be a lady
> ENSEMBLE:
Luck be a lady, roll will ya, roll will ya, what's
   the matter? Roll the dice!
> SKY:
Luck be a lady tonight.
> ENSEMBLE:
Comin' out, coming' out, comin' out, coming'
   out right.
> SKY, ENSEMBLE:
Ha!
Blackout.

4

A Street Off Broadway

Stage lights dim up.

Two Crap Shooters enter from R. One is putting on his tie. They exit L. Big Jule and Harry the Horse enter from R. They stop at stage R.C.

BIG JULE: I tell you I don't want to go to no prayer meeting.

HARRY: Big Jule, you give your marker, and if you welch, it will cause me no little embarrassment. I am sure you do not wish to cause me embarrassment?

They both walk to stage L. and stop.

BIG JULE: But if it ever gets back to Chicago that I went to a prayer meeting, no decent person will talk to me.

They exit L. Three Crap Shooters enter from R. and cross to stage L. Adelaide enters from L. reading a newspaper, she looks around, obviously looking for Nathan. She stops stage L. Nathan enters R. Adelaide sees him and drops the newspaper and purposely bumps into Nathan, Crap Shooter picks up newspaper as they exit L.

NATHAN: Adelaide!

ADELAIDE *Lady Windermere:* Oh! What a coincidence!

NATHAN: Adelaide, did Nicely explain to you about tonight? I hope you ain't sore about it?
Tries to embrace her, she pulls away to C.

ADELAIDE: Please! Let us not have a vulgar scene. After all, we are civilized people, we do not have to conduct ourselves like a slob.

NATHAN: Adelaide! What is this? You are my doll.

ADELAIDE: Your doll! Please, if that weren't so amusing one could laugh at it.

NATHAN: Sweetheart! Baby! How can you carry on like this over one lousy elopement? Adelaide, please!

ADELAIDE: It's no use, Nathan. I have succeeded in your not being able to upset me no more. I have got you completely out of my – *Sneezes. Then thows herself into Nathan's arms, weeping.* Oh, Nathan!

NATHAN: Adelaide, baby! Don't ever do that to me again! I can't stand it. We'll get married. We'll have a little home, a little white house with a green fence, just like the Whitney colours.

ADELAIDE *Through her tears:* Nathan, we got to do it soon. I had another letter from my mother today asking a lot of questions. And she put in a letter for you, too, *Hands it to him.*

NATHAN: A letter for me? From your mother? Well – *Opens it and reads.* . . . 'Dear Son Nathan: This is my first letter to you, although you have now been

married to my daughter for twelve years. But I feel like I know you from Adelaide's letters, and in my mind's eye I can see you as you go down to work every morning at seven. What a responsibility it must be, to be the assistant manager of an A. & P' *He breaks off.* I'm not even the manager? *Looks at Adelaide.*

ADELAIDE: I was going to promote you for Christmas.

NATHAN *Back to the letter:* . . . 'I know how hard you have to work to take care of your family, Adelaide and the five children and the one that's on the way.' *Looks at Adelaide.*

ADELAIDE: Mother wanted me to visit her, so I had to tell her that.

NATHAN *Righteous indignation:* Don't she know I can't have six kids on what they pay me at the A. & P.? *Reads quickly to himself, then slows up as he reads it aloud.* . . . 'I am very proud to have you as a son-in-law. You are a good man and I know you will always take care of Adelaide.' I feel like a heel.

ADELAIDE: Look, Nathan darling, we can still make everything all right. Look, it's not even midnight yet. Five minutes to twelve, let's elope right now.

NATHAN: Okay, Adelaide. *Embrace.*
Benny and Nicely enter from R. Nathan sees them.
No, I can't.

ADELAIDE: Why not?
Benny and Nicely are crossing at this moment.

BENNY: Come on, Nathan, we'll be late.

NICELY: Come on!
They exit L.

ADELAIDE *In measured tones:* Nathan, *why* can't we elope now?

NATHAN: Because, well, I got to go to a prayer meeting.

ADELAIDE *This one really hits her:* Nathan. This is the biggest lie you ever told me.

NATHAN: But I promise you it's true.

SUE ME

Adelaide takes letter from Nathan, tears letter up, throws it on floor, crosses D.R. Nathan kneels, picks up pieces of torn letter.

ADELAIDE:
You promise me this
You promise me that
You promise me anything under the sun
Then you give me a kiss
And you're grabbin' your hat
And you're off to the races again.
When I think of the time gone by.

NATHAN:
Adelaide! Adelaide! *(crosses to L. to her).*

ADELAIDE:
And I think of the way I try.

NATHAN:
Adelaide! *Adelaide crosses to L., pass Nathan.*

ADELAIDE:
I could honestly die.

NATHAN:
Call a lawyer and
Sue me, sue me,
What can you do me?
I love you
Give a holler and hate me, hate me,
Go ahead hate me
I love you.

ADELAIDE:
The best years of my life I was a fool to give to
   you.

NATHAN:
Alright, already I'm just a no goodnick
Alright already it's true, so nu?
So sue me, sue me
What can you do me?
I love you.
Tries to take her in his arms, she backs away to R.

ADELAIDE:
You gamble it here
You gamble it there
You gamble on everything all except me
And I'm sick of you keeping me up in the air
Till you're back in the money again
When I think of the time gone by.

NATHAN:
Adelaide! Adelaide!
ADELAIDE:
And I think of the way I try.
NATHAN:
Adelaide! *Crosses to Adelaide.*
ADELAIDE:
I could honestly die.
Backs away.

NATHAN:
Serve a paper and sue me, sue me,
What can you do me?
I love you. *She sneezes.*
Give a holler and hate me, hate me,
Go ahead hate me
I love you.
ADELAIDE *Crosses to L. pass him:*
When you wind up in jail don't come to me to
   bail you out.
NATHAN:
Alright, already so call a policeman,
Alright, already it's true, so nu?
She goes to him.
So sue me, sue me *They embrace.*
What can you do me?
I love you.
*Benny and Nicely enter from L. They beckon to
Nathan – Nathan waves them away. Adelaide turns
and sees them. They see the anger in her eyes and
hurriedly exit L.*
ADELAIDE *Crosses to R.:*
You're at it again.
You're running the game
I'm not gonna play second fiddle to that
And I'm sick and I'm tired of stalling around.
And I'm telling you now that we're through
When I think of the time gone by.
NATHAN *Crosses to her:*
Adelaide! Adelaide!
She waves him away:
ADELAIDE:
And I think of the way I try.
NATHAN:
Adelaide!
ADELAIDE:
I could honestly die.
NATHAN:
Sue me, sue me,
Shoot bullets through me
I love you.
She exits R. He exits L.

5

Interior of the Save-A-Soul Mission

The Mission Group ... Sarah, Arvide, Agatha and Calvin ... sits expectantly at a long table. A new figure is present ... The General. She is pacing the room, looking at the group who are momentarily growing more uneasy. Three benches and three chairs are at stage R.

GENERAL: It is now several minutes past midnight. Isn't anyone coming? Sergeant Sarah, something is very wrong.

ARVIDE: Maybe your watch is fast.

SARAH *Rises:* General I know what's wrong. *I'm* wrong. I've failed. I've spoken to these people day after day, but my words haven't reached them ... I think you had better ...
Mugs enter ... Sarah turns to them as they enter. Arvide rises.

ARVIDE *Sits:* Welcome, brothers. Welcome.
A few little grunts from the boys, then Sky enters.

SKY: Everybody here? Where's Nathan Detroit?
Nathan enters.

NATHAN: Present.

SKY *Crosses down C.:* Well Miss Sarah, here you are. One dozen or more assorted sinners. I'm sorry I didn't have time to clean 'em up for you.

ARVIDE *Rises:* Won't you gentlemen sit down?
They shuffle their feet a little.

HARRY: That's all right, we'll stand up.

SKY: Sit down! All of you.
They do.

Sarah sits in chair, Big Jule looks at General disgustedly. General crosses to left. Sits at table.

ARVIDE: Gentlemen, I would like to welcome you to the Save-A-Soul Mission.
A loud Bronx cheer from one of the gang.

Arvide sits.

SKY: Just a minute, you guys. This is a Mission, not a Saloon, and I suggest that you do not indulge in any unpleasantness. Since I am required to depart for points West to-night ...
Sarah moves.
... I am appointing Nathan Detroit Major Domo in my place. Nathan, anybody who does not conduct himself according to Hoyle will answer to Sky Masterson personally, and that means in person.
He gives them a final glance, then goes, exits L.

GENERAL *From the silence:* What a remarkable young man!
Sarah looks at her, but says nothing.

NATHAN *Rises, confronts them, clears his throat and shouts:* So remember that, you guys. *Turns to Arvide.* Brother Abernathy, your dice. *He sits.*

ARVIDE *Rises:* Gentlemen, to-night we are honoured. Our meeting will be conducted by the head of our organization. General Cartwright. *Sits.*

Nathan starts the applause.

GENERAL *Rises:* Gentlemen, it is wonderful to see our Mission graced by the presence of so many evil-looking sinners.

Nathan starts to applaud, but realizes he may be wrong.

Now, who would like to testify? Who would like to start the ball rolling by giving testimony?

They are silent and hang their heads.

NATHAN: Benny! Give testimony.

BENNY: I ain't no stool pigeon.

GENERAL: Come, brothers, I know it is difficult. But let one of you give testimony to the sin that is in his heart.

NATHAN: Benny! Tell 'em what a bum you are.

Benny rises.

Benny!

BENNY *Forced to it:* I always was a bad guy, and a gambler, but I ain't going to do it no more. I thank you. *Sits quickly.*

GENERAL: There! Don't you feel better now?

BENNY: I'm alright.

GENERAL: Anyone else?

NATHAN: Big Jule.

BIG JULE: What's the pitch?

NATHAN: Just tell them about all the terrible things you done but ain't going to do no more.

BIG JULE *Rises:* Well, I used to be bad when I was a kid, but ever since then I have gone straight as I can prove by my record, thirty-three arrests and no convictions. *Sits.*

NATHAN *Pointing:* Harry!

HARRY: Oh, No!

NATHAN: Oh yes. *Louder this time.* Harry the Horse!

HARRY *Getting reluctantly to his feet*: Ah, well, like when Sky rolled us for our souls . . .

GENERAL: I beg your pardon?

HARRY: Sky Masterson, he rolled us a thousand dollars against our souls. That's why we're here.

GENERAL: I don't think I understand.

SARAH: I do, General. He means that they are only here because Mr. Masterson won them in a dice game.

GENERAL: How wonderful! This whole meeting the result of gambling! It shows how good can come out of evil. *Pounds table.* Sergeant Sarah, you have done remarkable work.

ARVIDE: Hasn't she though?

SARAH: Thank you.

HARRY: Hey! I ain't finished my testimony. Well my sin is that when Sky rolled us I wished I would win the thousand dollars instead of having to

come here but now that I'm here I still wish it. *Sits.*

GENERAL: Anybody else?

Brannigan plunges in from L. ready for anything; he points to Nathan. Nathan raises a warning finger to his lips.

Brannigan subsides. Nathan removes Brannigan's hat and places over his extended finger.

NATHAN *In a new voice of piety:* We will now hear testimony from – *He looks them over.* Brother Nicely-Nicely Johnson.

Nicely forces a smile, then Nathan sweetly says: Brother Nicely-Nicely Johnson –

BIG JULE: Get up, you fat water buffalo.

Nicely slowly rises.

NICELY: Well. It happened to me kind of funny. Like a dream. That's it, a dream.

GENERAL: Tell it in your own words.

She sits. Nicely places his hat on chair. Nathan points to chair up C. which Brannigan sits in. Nathan sits in his chair.

SIT DOWN, YOU'RE ROCKIN' THE BOAT

NICELY:
I dreamed last night I got on a boat to Heaven
And by some chance I had brought my dice along
And there I stood
And I hollered 'Someone fade me'
But the passengers, they knew right from wrong.
For the people all said sit down, sit down, you're rockin' the boat.

ENSEMBLE:
People all said sit down, sit down, you're rockin' the boat.

NICELY:
And the devil will drag you under
By the sharp lapel of your checkered coat
Sit down, sit down, sit down, sit down,

ENSEMBLE:
Sit down, you're rockin' the boat.

NICELY:
I sailed away on that little boat to Heaven
And by some chance found a bottle in my fist.

ENSEMBLE:
Ooo –

NICELY:
And there I stood.

ENSEMBLE:
Ooo –

NICELY:
Nicely passin' out the whiskey
But the passengers were bound to resist

ENSEMBLE:
Ooo –

NICELY:
For the people all said beware, you're on a heavenly trip.

ENSEMBLE:
People all said beware – beware.

NICELY:
People all said beware, beware, you'll scuttle the ship.

ENSEMBLE:
People all said beware.

NICELY:
And the devil will drag you under.
They all rise.

ENSEMBLE:
Sit down –

NICELY:
By the fancy tie 'round your wicked throat
Sit down, sit down, sit down, sit down.

ENSEMBLE:
Sit down, sit down.
They all sit down.

NICELY:
Sit down, you're rockin' the boat.

ENSEMBLE:
Sit down, you're rockin' the boat – Down –

NICELY:
And as I laughed at those passengers to
    Heaven.
Laughs.
Gasps.
    A great big wave came and washed me
    overboard.
ENSEMBLE:
Ooo –
NICELY:
And as I sank.
ENSEMBLE:
Ooo –
NICELY:
And I hollered 'Someone save me.' –
That's the moment I woke up.
ENSEMBLE:
Ooo –
NICELY:
Thank the Lord.
ENSEMBLE *Mission band rises:*
Thank the Lord, thank the Lord.
NICELY:
And I said to myself, sit down, sit down,
    You're rockin' the boat.
ENSEMBLE:
Said to himself sit down, sit down.
NICELY:
Said to myself, sit down, sit down, you're
    rockin' the boat.
ENSEMBLE *Mission band sits:*
Said to himself sit down.
NICELY:
And the devil will drag you under.
ENSEMBLE:
And the devil will drag you under.
NICELY:
With a soul so heavy you'd never float,
Sit down.
NICELY AND ENSEMBLE:
Sit down, sit down, sit down,
Sit down, you're rockin' the boat.
They all rise, slowly till end.
NICELY AND ENSEMBLE *Ending:*
Sit down, you're rocking', sit down, sit down,
Sit down, you're rockin' the boat.
Sit down, you're rockin', sit down, sit down,
Sit down, you're rockin' the boat.
Sit down, you're rockin' the boat.

At end of number Nathan and Brannigan rise.
NATHAN: Well Brother Brannigan, what can we do
    for you. Maybe you would care to testify?

BRANNIGAN: I'll do my testifying in court, where I
    will testify that you ran a crap game here in the
    Mission last night. Miss Sarah, you were standing
    there when they came out. You saw them. Aren't
    these the fellows?
SARAH *Slowly looks at them; takes her time:* I never
    saw them before in my life.
BIG JULE: There's a right broad.
ARVIDE *Rises:* Now if you would excuse us officer, we
    would like to go on with our meeting.
BRANNIGAN: I never saw crap shooters spend so
    much time in a Mission. Maybe that's what they
    mean by Holy Rollers.
    *He puts his hat on and exits L. Harry the Horse rises
    indignantly. Nathan waves him down as Big Jule
    pulls Harry down by the sleeve.*
NATHAN: Thank you Miss Sarah . . . People, I also
    got a confession to make, and I got to get it off my
    chest. It is true that we did shoot crap here last
    night, but we're all sorry. Ain't we, boys?
    *He turns to the mob, they mumble assents: hanging of
    heads.*
BIG JULE: I'm really sorry.
NATHAN *Turning to Sarah:* But I done another terrible
    thing. *Crosses down C.* I made a bet with a certain
    guy that he could not take a certain doll away with
    him on a trip, and this I should not have done,
    although it did not do no harm, as I won the bet.
SARAH: You won the bet?
NATHAN: Sure. The guy told me that he did not take
    the doll. Well, that makes me feel a lot better.
GENERAL *Rises:* Hallelujah!
NATHAN: Hallelujah! *Sits.*
    *The mob all say Hallelujah. General picks up and
    hands out song books.*
GENERAL: Gentlemen, we will now sing No. 244.
    'FOLLOW THE FOLD'.
    *She stands in front of them and raises hand and con-
    ducts. Music begins. Sarah quietly picks up cape exits.*

6

Near Times Square

Two roped together bundles of newspaper tabloids on which two people can sit are stage C.

Adelaide enters, disconsolately from R. Drops on to newspaper bundles R.C., sneezes. A passing Male enters from stage L. stops to look at her to flirt, if encouraged.

ADELAIDE *Angrily:* Oh, go away!

    He hurries off R. Adelaide starts to sing softly as Sarah enters singing softly from stage L. She is wearing a cape, she sits on newspaper bundle L.C. not noticing Adelaide.

ADELAIDE Singing:

'Keep the Vicks on your chest
And get plenty of rest'
You can wisely warn her
But, in spite of the quiet,
Massages and diet,
She's still a goner
Once she gets the idea that the little
Church will always be around the corner
A person can develop a cold. *Looks at Sarah.*

SARAH Singing:

So please forgive this
Helpless haze I'm in
I've never really been in love before.

ADELAIDE *Noticing Sarah and not caring much:* Oh, hello.

SARAH *Uncertainly:* Good evening.

ADELAIDE: I'm Adelaide, the well known fiancée.

SARAH: Oh, yes. When are you getting married?

ADELAIDE: The twelfth of never.

SARAH: Oh, I'm sorry.

ADELAIDE: I didn't even get close enough to a church to be left at it . . . *Half to herself.* Gee, what'll I ever tell my mother?

SARAH: Oh, your mother will understand. Just tell her your engagement is broken.

ADELAIDE *Gives her a look:* I'm afraid that might confuse her . . . Maybe I'll tell her Nathan is dead, and then see *to* it.

SARAH: You mustn't carry hate in your heart, Miss Adelaide. Try to be forgiving and understanding, and the pain will go away. In the Bible it tells us in Isaiah . . . Isaiah . . . *The thought is too much for her* . . . Isaiah . . . *But she cannot go ahead.*

ADELAIDE: You've got a boy friend named Isaiah, huh?

SARAH *Through her tears:* Isaiah was an ancient prophet.

ADELAIDE: Don't tell me. Nobody cries like that over an old guy . . . Whoever it is, you got it bad. You know, when I saw you with Sky Masterson the other night –

Sarah goes into a fresh outburst of tears. Adelaide looks at her.

– Oh, no! Not Sky! You're not in love with Sky? *No answer which is its own confirmation.* You poor thing!

Sarah gestures helplessly.

SARAH *Low voiced:* I thought I hated him.

ADELAIDE: I thought I hated Nathan. I still think I hate him. That's love.

SARAH: Adelaide, can't men like Sky ever change?

ADELAIDE *Shakes her head:* For fourteen years I've tried to change Nathan. I've always thought how wonderful he would be, if he was different.

SARAH: I've thought about Sky that way, too.

ADELAIDE: I've sat and pictured him by the hour. Nathan, my Nathan, in a little home in the country . . . happy . . .

Lights go on behind her R. revealing a Nathan in overalls and farmer's hat, standing beside a trellis of beautiful roses. With a spray gun he is tenderly treating each bud with loving care. He picks off a bug; removes his hat to wipe his brow. The lights go down again.

ADELAIDE *Sighs as picture fades:* Gee, wouldn't it be wonderful.

SARAH: Wouldn't it. If only Sky . . .

On the other side Sky now appears L. He appears as in Sarah's imagination. He is wearing a dainty bib-type kitchen apron, holding wicker laundry basket filled with diapers. With clothes-pins in his mouth he is hanging diapers on line. The vision fades.

ADELAIDE *Sigh:* But they just can't change.

SARAH: A little while ago at our prayer meeting there were a lot of gamblers who acted as though maybe they could change.

ADELAIDE: Yes, but that doesn't mean . . . gamblers at your prayer meeting . . . was Nathan Detroit there?

SARAH: I'm sure I heard that name.

ADELAIDE: A darling little fellow with a cute moustache?

SARAH: I think so.

ADELAIDE *Rises, crosses down C:* How do you like that rat! Just when he should have been lying he's telling the truth! I'm glad I'm through with him. *Turns to Sarah.* And you ought to be glad you're through with Sky, too.

SARAH *Thoughtfully:* I am.

Two girls look at each other for a moment.

ADELAIDE *Crosses to Sarah, sits on bundle of newspapers:* What are we – crazy or something?

MARRY THE MAN TODAY

ADELAIDE *Spoken:*
At Wanamaker's and Sak's and Klein's
Sung: A lesson I've been taught
You can't get alterations on a dress you haven't
Why not?

SARAH:
At any veg'table market from Borneo to Nome
You mustn't squeeze a melon till you get the
    melon home.

ADELAIDE:
You've simply got to gamble *Looks at Sarah*.

SARAH:
You get no guarantee.

ADELAIDE:
Now doesn't that kind of apply to you and I?

SARAH:
You and me.

ADELAIDE *Spoken. Rises:*
Why not?

SARAH *Spoken. Rises:*
Why not what?

ADELAIDE *Sings. Two steps D. front:*
Marry the man today
Sarah moves down alongside of her. Two steps D.S.

Trouble though he may be
Much as he loves to play
Crazy and wild and free.

SARAH AND ADELAIDE:
Marry the man today (*walks D.S. 1 step*).
Turn to one another.

Rather than sigh and sorrow

ADELAIDE:
Marry the man today
And change his ways tomorrow (*crosses 3 steps
    R.*).

SARAH:
Marry the man today
Maybe he's leaving town
Pulls Adelaide back.

Don't let him get away
Motions with fist.

Hurry and track him down

ADELAIDE:
Marry the man today
Moving S.R.
Maybe he's leaving town
Don't let him get away
Counter-attack him and
SARAH AND ADELAIDE:
Marry the man today
Both put hands out.
Give him the girlish laughter.
SARAH:
Give him your hand today and
Save the fist for after
ADELAIDE *Crosses to R.:*
Slowly introduce him to the better things
Respectable, conservative and clean.
SARAH *Crosses to Adelaide:*
Readers Digest!
ADELAIDE: Guy Lombardo!
SARAH: Rogers Peet!
ADELAIDE *(spoken):* Golf!
SARAH *(spoken):* Galoshes!
ADELAIDE *Sung:*
Ovaltine! *Sarah nods.*
BOTH:
But marry the man today
Fist gesture
Handle it meek and gently.
ADELAIDE *Crosses to Sarah:*
Marry the man today and train him
subsequently.
SARAH:
Carefully expose him to domestic life
And if he ever tries to stray from you
Have a pot-roast.
ADELAIDE:
Have a headache.
Hand to head.
SARAH:
Have a baby.
ADELAIDE:
Have two!
SARAH *Spoken:* Six!
ADELAIDE *Spoken:* Nine!
SARAH *Spoken:* Stop!
BOTH *Sung*
Marry the man today
Rather than sigh and sorrow
Marry the man today
They shake hands.
And change his ways, and change his ways,
and change his ways tomorrow!
*Adelaide exits R. Sarah exits L. They pound their
fists as they exit.*

7

Broadway

The two Broadway characters we saw in opening scene are discovered at stage C. doing the same routine as the lights dim up and Show Trans. Traveller opens. The two street walkers are at the newsstand and cross over to the two Broadway characters who turn them down and exit R. followed by the two street walkers.

All the Mugs march on from L. They have been cleaned up, and each one is wearing a big white Gardenia. Harry is in the lead followed by Nicely, Benny. They stand in line.

The Paper Doll Vendor and his Assistant enter from R. and set up their pitch stage C. The Prizefighter and his Manager watch the bouncing doll and the Prizefighter motions to his Manager to buy one which he does. The Prizefighter places the doll stage C. to watch it bounce but it collapses. He picks it up in disgust. All the mugs cross to stage R.

Sightseeing Crowd enter from R. and stand up C.

Brannigan enters from L. and goes to newsstand which is strung with Christmas tree lights and stands in front of it looking at the lights.

Adelaide enters from R. followed by Girls. She is dressed in a wedding outfit and carries a bouquet in her hands. She is very nervous and calls off L. . . .

ADELAIDE: Nathan! Nathan! Where are you! Nathan!

BRANNIGAN *At newsstand:* Gimme a late paper.

ADELAIDE: Nathan darling, come on, we're waiting for you.
Nathan sticks his head out of the newsstand. He is wearing a red turtle neck sweater.

NATHAN: Just a minute! I'm waiting on the Lieutenant . . . Thank you, Lieutenant.

ADELAIDE: Nathan, close up the newsstand. We're getting married.
Nathan pulls down shade on newsstand. On it is painted 'Nathan Detroit's NewsStand'.

HARRY *Crosses to C.:* Look, is this wedding going to take place or ain't it? I paid a half a buck for this Mesanthecrum.

ADELAIDE *Shouting to newsstand:* Nathan! Come on.
Nathan emerges through a small door at R. end of newsstand. He is carrying a top hat, and cane in his hand and is wearing a very elegant cut-away outfit.

NATHAN *Crosses to Adelaide:* Gee, Adelaide, you picked the busiest time of the day.

HARRY *Crosses in two steps:* Let's go. Where's the wedding?

NATHAN: Holy smoke!

ADELAIDE: What's the matter?

NATHAN *Crosses to R. pass Adelaide:* I forgot to get a place for the wedding.

ADELAIDE: Oh, Nathan!

NICELY: How about the Biltmore Garage?
Mission Band enters playing.
All five of the Mission Band . . . for who is now a member but Mr. Sky Masterson! And in uniform, too. He is ripping out 'FOLLOW THE FOLD' with the rest of them, swinging his big drum stick lustily. Arvide, meanwhile, has shifted to the cymbals. They stop playing as they get to stage C.

SKY *Starting the pitch, crosses downstage one step:* Brothers and Sisters! *Bangs drum.* Life is one big crap game and the Devil is using loaded dice!

BIG JULE *Enters from R.:* Where's the crap game?

NATHAN *Hits drum with cane.* Brother Masterson?

SKY: What is it, Brother Detroit?

NATHAN: Is it O.K. if we get married in your Mission, Adelaide and I?
Sky looks at Sarah, who looks at Arvide.

ARVIDE: Certainly, I married Sister Sarah and Brother Masterson. Glad to do the same for you.

SKY: Congratulations, Nathan! I'll lay you eight to five you'll be very happy.

SARAH: What Obediah really means is –

NATHAN: Obediah?

SARAH: – he wishes you every happiness and so do I.

ADELAIDE: Thank you very much . . . I *know* we're going to be happy. We're going to have a little place in the country, and Nathan will be sitting there, beside me, every single night.
Comes an enormous sneeze from Nathan. Then her expression changes as she realizes its implications.

THE HAPPY ENDING – GUYS AND DOLLS
When you see a guy, reach for stars in the sky
You can bet that he's doing it for some doll
When you spot a John waiting out in the rain
Chances are he's insane as only a John can be
  for a Jane,
When you meet a gent paying all kinds of rent
For a flat that could flatten the Taj Mahal
Call it sad, call it funny, but it's better than
  even money.
  That the guys only doing it for some doll.
Curtain.